Cyberterrorism and Ransomware Attacks

Other Books in the Global Viewpoints Series

Arms Sales, Treaties, and Violations
Civilian Casualties in War
Economic Sanctions
Extreme Weather Events
Geoengineering
Hate Crimes
Honor Killings
Migrants and Refugees
Religious Clothing in Public Spaces
Revisiting Nuclear Power
Tech Giants and Digital Domination

Cyberterrorism and Ransomware Attacks

Gary Wiener, Book Editor

Published in 2019 by Greenhaven Publishing, LLC
353 3rd Avenue, Suite 255, New York, NY 10010

First Edition

Articles in Greenhaven Publishing anthologies are often edited for length to meet page requirements. In addition, original titles of these works are changed to clearly present the main thesis and to explicitly indicate the author's opinion. Every effort is made to ensure that Greenhaven Publishing accurately reflects the original intent of the authors. Every effort has been made to trace the owners of the copyrighted material.

Cover image: Alexander Ryumin\TASS via Getty Images

Library of Congress Cataloging-in-Publication Data

Names: Wiener, Gary, editor.
Title: Cyberterrorism and ransomware attacks / Gary Wiener, book editor.
Description: First edition. | New York : Greenhaven Publishing, 2019. | Series: Global viewpoints | Includes bibliographical references and index. | Audience: Grades 9–12.
Identifiers: LCCN 2018004923| ISBN 9781534503403 (library bound) | ISBN 9781534503410 (pbk.)
Subjects: LCSH: Cyberterrorism—Juvenile literature. | Extortion—Juvenile literature. | Computer crimes—Juvenile literature.
Classification: LCC HV6773.15.C97 C938 2019 | DDC 363.325—dc23
LC record available at https://lccn.loc.gov/2018004923

Manufactured in the United States of America

Website: http://greenhavenpublishing.com

Contents

Chapter 2: State-Sponsored Cyberterrorism

Chapter 3: Profiteering from Ransomware

Chapter 4: Combatting Cyberterrorism and Ransomware

Foreword

"The problems of all of humanity can only be solved by all of humanity."
—Swiss author Friedrich Dürrenmatt

Global interdependence has become an undeniable reality. Mass media and technology have increased worldwide access to information and created a society of global citizens. Understanding and navigating this global community is a challenge, requiring a high degree of information literacy and a new level of learning sophistication.

Building on the success of its flagship series, Opposing Viewpoints, Greenhaven Publishing has created the Global Viewpoints series to examine a broad range of current, often controversial topics of worldwide importance from a variety of international perspectives. Providing students and other readers with the information they need to explore global connections and think critically about worldwide implications, each Global Viewpoints volume offers a panoramic view of a topic of widespread significance.

Drugs, famine, immigration—a broad, international treatment is essential to do justice to social, environmental, health, and political issues such as these. Junior high, high school, and early college students, as well as general readers, can all use Global Viewpoints anthologies to discern the complexities relating to each issue. Readers will be able to examine unique national perspectives while, at the same time, appreciating the interconnectedness that global priorities bring to all nations and cultures.

Material in each volume is selected from a diverse range of sources, including journals, magazines, newspapers, nonfiction books, speeches, government documents, pamphlets, organization newsletters, and position papers. Global Viewpoints is truly global, with material drawn primarily from international sources available in English and secondarily from US sources with extensive international coverage.

Features of each volume in the Global Viewpoints series include:

- An **annotated table of contents** that provides a brief summary of each essay in the volume, including the name of the country or area covered in the essay.
- An **introduction** specific to the volume topic.
- A **world map** to help readers locate the countries or areas covered in the essays.
- For each viewpoint, an **introduction** that contains notes about the author and source of the viewpoint explains why material from the specific country is being presented, summarizes the main points of the viewpoint, and offers three **guided reading questions** to aid in understanding and comprehension.
- **For further discussion questions** that promote critical thinking by asking the reader to compare and contrast aspects of the viewpoints or draw conclusions about perspectives and arguments.
- A worldwide list of **organizations to contact** for readers seeking additional information.
- A **periodical bibliography** for each chapter and a **bibliography of books** on the volume topic to aid in further research.
- A comprehensive **subject index** to offer access to people, places, events, and subjects cited in the text.

Global Viewpoints is designed for a broad spectrum of readers who want to learn more about current events, history, political science, government, international relations, economics, environmental science, world cultures, and sociology—students doing research for class assignments or debates, teachers and faculty seeking to supplement course materials, and others wanting to understand current issues better. By presenting how people in various countries perceive the root causes, current consequences, and proposed solutions to worldwide challenges, Global Viewpoints volumes offer readers opportunities to enhance their global awareness and their knowledge of cultures worldwide.

Introduction

> *"Tomorrow's terrorist may be able to do more damage with a keyboard than with a bomb."*
>
> *— National Research Council, Computers at Risk (1991)*

The first question that arises when considering cyberterrorism is one of definition. The term "cyberterrorism" itself was first coined by Barry C. Collin, a senior researcher at the Institute for Security and Intelligence in California, who noted the convergence of cybernetics and terrorism in the 1990s. But exactly what is cyberterrorism, and who is a cyberterrorist? Such definitions vary depending on who is asked. This is in part due to the difficulty of defining terrorism itself, as experts have continually disagreed with each other on the subject. A famous saying holds that "One man's terrorist is another's freedom fighter."

Cybersecurity analyst Ryan Littlefield wrote that "By definition cyber terrorism means to damage information, computer systems and data that result in harm against non-combatant targets." However, he added, "the boundaries between acts of cyber terrorism, cyber crime and 'Hacktivism' are often interlinked."[1]

One particularly vivid response is attributed to Collin himself, who maintained that cyberterrorism is "hacking" with a body count.

The United States Department of Defense (DOD) defines terrorism as "the calculated use of unlawful violence or threat of unlawful violence to inculcate fear, intended to coerce or to intimidate governments or societies in the pursuit of goals that are generally political, religious, or ideological."[2]

Just how murky the issue of cyberterrorism is can be made clear by two contrasting examples. When, in 2014, North Korea retaliated against Sony Pictures through cyberattack over the forthcoming release of a Seth Rogan-James Franco movie *The Interview*, whose premise was an assassination attempt on North Korean leader Kim Jong-Un, many were quick to label it as cyberterrorism. "The Sony hack is indicative of a new breed of terrorism targeting our companies, our citizens, and our way of life," wrote Nathaniel Beach-Westmoreland in *Wired* magazine.[3] Conversely, when the United States unleashed the Stuxnet virus against Iranian computers running their uranium-enrichment program in 2010, virtually nobody considered the United States' actions cyberterrorism: except the Iranians, of course.

Iran's reaction was to fight fire with fire. In the years following Stuxnet, the Iranian government is the chief suspect in cyber attacks on Saudi state oil company Aramco; the Qatari natural gas firm RasGas in 2012; and the Las Vegas, Nevada, Sands casino in 2014. Iranian hackers were also thought to be responsible for a cyberattack on United States banks in 2012. "Iran's response to Stuxnet cost millions of dollars to our financial sector and presumably they could wreak worse havoc if provoked," said Barbara Slavin, Nonresident Senior Fellow in the Atlantic Council's South Asia Center.[4]

It is still an open question, however, as to whether state-sponsored cyberattacks constitute terrorism, or if they are simply cyberwar. In an article entitled, "State Cyberterrorism: A Contradiction in Terms?" Lee Jarvis, Stuart Macdonald, and Lella Nouri argue that "that there exists considerable 'expert' support for the validity of the proposition that states can indeed engage in cyberterrorism," and that whether states are deemed capable of cyberterrorism has implications for subsidiary debates, including around the threat that cyberterrorism poses.[5]

What is not disputed is that cyberterrorism poses an increasing danger in today's ever-expanding technological world. As far back as in 1991, the National Research Council foresaw the coming problem: "Tomorrow's terrorist may be able to do more damage with a keyboard than with a bomb," it wrote.[6] With technology continually developing new ways to harness the power of the internet—both for good and for bad—the possibilities for cyber chaos become increasingly real.

In particular, the advent of the internet of things (IoT) has broadened the possibilities for cyberterrorism. "The internet of things is a blanket term used to describe our increasingly connected world," writes Tony Bradley for *PCWorld*. "Refrigerators, thermostats, cars, smoke detectors, watches, glasses, and just about every other appliance you can think of is being connected to the Internet to provide remote access or to monitor and collected data."[7]

And while people are not likely to experience a cyber terror attack on their internet-linked doorbells, the possibility for ransomware attacks on the internet of things is not far-fetched. Imagine the destructive and even life-threatening possibilities if hackers can take control of a vehicle, or a number of vehicles, on roads and highways. Today, terrorists often attack by using vehicles to plow down pedestrians in crowded cities such as London and New York. What if this could be done from a distance, with a far-off cyberterrorist taking control of cars or trucks?

Many people now have thermostats linked to the internet. Some have even granted access to their power companies to lower or raise the temperature in their houses during periods of peak use (especially on very hot days). But what if terrorists were able to lower the thermostat temperature in thousands or even millions of houses simultaneously during a heat wave? What would be the effect on the electrical grid and on a power company itself? Such questions, unthinkable even a few years ago, must now be considered by corporations and governments worldwide. As Bradley writes, "IoT has tremendous potential to enhance our standard of living, but it also introduces substantial risk for devices that were previously immune from such threats."[8]

It should come as no surprise then, that corporations and governments are currently addressing the cyberterrorism threat.

But are there efforts, always limited by time and money, enough to ward off existential threats to the way people live today? Only the future will decide for sure if the white hats (good guys) or black hats (bad guys) win in the new cyberterrorism wars. The viewpoints in *Global Viewpoints: Cyberterrorism and Ransomware* explore dangers from individuals, groups, and governments, and the emerging threat of ransomware. The authors of the viewpoints in this volume also investigate what individuals, corporations, and governments can do to remain safe in an ever-more-dangerous internet environment.

Endnotes

1. Quoted in Mohammed Iqbal, "Defining Cyberterrorism." *The John Marshall Journal of Information Technology & Privacy Law*. Winter 2004. 22:2. p. 397.
2. Quoted in Irving Lachow, "Cyber Terrorism: Menace or Myth?" in *Cyberpower and National Security*, ed. Franklin D. Kramer, Stuart H. Starr, and Larry K. Wentz. Washington D.C.: National Defense University Press, 2009. p. 437.
3. Nathaniel Beach-Westmoreland, "If North Korea Did Hack Sony, It's a Whole New Kind of Cyberterrorism." *Wired*. December 23, 2014. https://www.wired.com/2014/12/why-america-must-answer-north-korea/
4. Quoted in Ashish Kumar Sen, "Iran's Growing Cyber Capabilities in a Post-Stuxnet Era." *Atlantic Council*. April 10, 2015. http://www.atlanticcouncil.org/blogs/newatlanticist/iran-s-growing-cyber-capabilities-in-a-post-stuxnet-era
5. Lee Jarvis, Stuart Macdonald, and Lella Nouri, "State Cyberterrorism: A Contradiction in Terms?" *Journal of Terrorism Research*. 2015. 6(3), p. 62. http://doi.org/10.15664/jtr.1162
6. Quoted in LathaSubrananian, Jianhong Liu, and John Winterdyk, "Cyber-Terrorism and Cyber Security: A Global Perspective." *ResearchGate*. October 11, 2016. https://www.researchgate.net/publication/308983209_CyberTerrorism_and_Cyber_Security_A_Global_Perspective
7. Tony Bradley, "How the Internet of Things opens your home to cyber threats. *PCWorld*. March 3, 2014. https://www.pcworld.com/article/2103143/how-the-internet-of-things-opens-your-home-to-cyber-threats.html
8. Ibid.

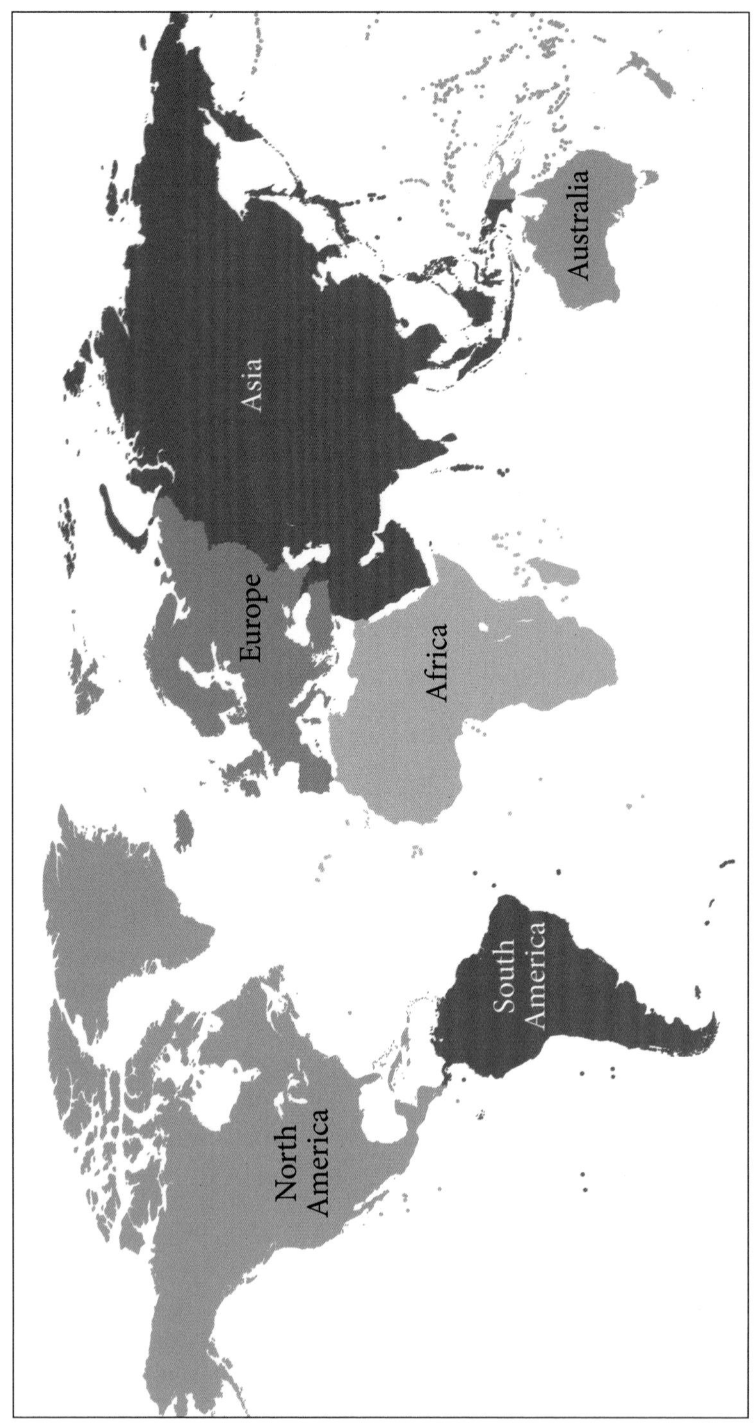
Asia
Australia
Europe
Africa
South America
North America

Chapter 1

Cyberterrorism Around the World

Viewpoint 1

Terrorism Enabled by Cyber Criminals Is Our Most Likely Major Cyber Threat

Steven Bucci

There are numerous cyber threats in today's world. In the following viewpoint, Steven Bucci categorizes these threats into low, medium, and high levels of danger, the highest being perpetrated by nation-states. But internet terrorism by actual terrorist groups, while still not common, is a looming high-level threat as well. If terrorists are able to harness the power of cyber criminals, the consequences could be dire. Steven Bucci, who formerly served as an Army Special Forces officer and top Pentagon official, is a visiting fellow in The Heritage Foundation's Allison Center for Foreign Policy Studies, where he focuses on cybersecurity, military special operations, and defense support to civil authorities.

As you read, consider the following questions:

1. What are the different "levels of danger" that Bucci discusses?
2. Why are threats from nation-states the most serious?
3. To date, how have terrorists used the internet to further their aims? What have they not been able to do?

"The Confluence of Cyber Crime and Terrorism," by Steven Bucci, Heritage Foundation, June 12, 2009. Reprinted by permission.

Today the world faces a wide array of cyber threats. The majority of these threats are aimed at the Western democracies and the Western-leaning countries of other regions.

The reason for this is simple: They are ripe targets. These countries are either highly dependent, almost completely in some cases, on cyber means for nearly every significant societal interaction or are racing toward that goal. They seek the speed, accuracy, efficiency, and ease that a "wired" system of systems brings and all the benefits that accrue to such a situation.

The danger we face is that there are many individuals, groups, and states that desire to exploit those same systems for their own purposes. There is a new threat on the horizon that must be recognized and addressed.

Cyber threats we face today can be grouped into seven categories that form a spectrum of sorts. Any of these threat groups can attack an individual, a nation-state, and anything in between. They will exploit a lazy home computer user, an inefficient corporate information technology system, or a weak national infrastructure defense.

Levels of Danger

We are all in danger from these threats, which can be grouped as low, medium, and high levels of danger. Any construct of this nature is a simplification, but it does aid in discussions to have the numerous possible actions defined into manageable groups.

At the low danger end, there are two groups of threats. The lowest level is the individual hacker. He operates for his own personal benefit: for pride, self-satisfaction, or individual financial gain. He constitutes an annoyance. The hacker category also includes small groups who write malware (malicious software) to prove that they can or who attack small organizations due to personal or political issues.

With the hacker at the low end of the spectrum are small criminal enterprises and most disgruntled insiders. These too are low-level annoyances, except for the unfortunate individuals they exploit as their primary targets. These operate Internet scams, bilking people out of personal information, and may even perpetrate extortion through threats.

Continuing along the spectrum, the medium-level threats are harder to break down in a rank order. Each threat grouping targets different entities. These targets would consider their attackers very dangerous and a critical threat. These medium-level threats include:

- Terrorist use of the Internet;
- Cyber espionage, which is also helped by insiders at times, both corporate and national security types, including probes for vulnerabilities and implementation of backdoors; and
- High-level organized crime.

Cyber Threat Spectrum

All three of these groupings can have extremely detrimental effects on a person, a business, a government, or a region. They occur regularly and define the ongoing significant threats we face every day.

The high-level threats involve the full power of nation-states. These come in two major groups. The first is a full-scale nation-state cyber attack. The closest example of this was the assault made on Estonia in 2007. There, the highly developed network of a small country was temporarily brought to its knees. Portrayed by some as a simple display of public outrage over the moving of a statue, most felt there was more going on and that a government hand was at play.

This dispute over the responsibility makes this an imperfect example, but it is a highly troubling harbinger of the future. One former Department of Defense (DoD) leader stated that over 1 million computers were used in this event, coming from over 70 countries.

The other possibility is the cyber enablement of a kinetic attack. So far, we can only look to the 2008 assault on Georgia to study this category. Georgia was not as dependent on the cyber realm as was

Estonia, but the cyber assault that preceded the Russian military's ground attack into Ossetia severely hindered Georgia's response. Again, it may be an imperfect example, but it has given us much to consider. The same former DoD official described it this way:

> [T]heir cyber special operations forces isolated the president by disabling all his cyber connectivity, then their cyber air force carpet bombed the entire national network, and finally their cyber Delta Force infiltrated and rewrote code that kept their network from working correctly even after it was brought back up. It was a highly sophisticated attack.

These two potential threats constitute the high end of the cyber-threat spectrum.

A Construct for Planning

During the Cold War and beyond, the military and security communities used a paradigm for planning that allowed them to determine against which of a large number of possible threats they should plan. They would determine both the most dangerous threat and the most likely threat. These were seldom the same.

During that period, there was near-universal agreement that full-scale thermonuclear exchange between the US and NATO on one side and the Soviet Union and the Warsaw Pact on the other was the most dangerous threat. Fortunately, this was not the most likely threat. Mutually assured destruction kept the fingers off the triggers.

Planners therefore had to ascertain what scenario was the most likely. For NATO, this was a large-scale conventional war on the plains of Northern Europe, which all hoped would remain non-nuclear. For the US, they added smaller-scale proxy wars outside the European context. Today, we can use a similar process to help us thoughtfully address cyber threats.

While we face a scenario emerging from the cyber-threat spectrum that fully fits the part of the most dangerous threat, we must also face and prepare for a most likely scenario that is unique and, frankly, is not yet on the cyber-threat spectrum. This threat will involve the joining of the growing cyber-crime capability we see today with the terrorists' realization that the cyber realm is ripe for exploitation and that joining with cyber criminals will be their path to that exploitation.

The Most Dangerous Cyber Threat: Nation-State Attacks

Clearly, as one looks at the spectrum of threats, the far end delineates the possibilities we fear most. Developed nation-states, acting as peer competitors, are the most dangerous potential threat.

Nation-states possess hard power, including kinetically capable militaries, economic strength, industrial bases, and scale of assets. They can marshal the intellectual capital to develop cyber armies—large numbers of operators with the best equipment, skilled at developing and using new forms of attack. These will do the twin tasks of both leveraging and enabling conventional intelligence, signals, and mobility assets.

Nation-states can also use their considerable coercive powers to harness civilian assets that technically fall outside the public sector. This can be done by requiring active or passive collusion with the government or by manipulating public sentiment to stir up patriotic fervor while providing guidance (i.e., targeting) and tools to the faithful.

All of the above factors allow nation-states with foresight to develop and use enormous capabilities in the cyber realm. What is today merely cyber espionage or probing of defenses can, in the blink of an eye, be turned into a massive attack on the infrastructure of an adversary.

Remember: Cyber forces do not need to deploy by ship, plane, or truck, so there are no logistical delays or the usual indicators and warnings. Cyber attacks could be used to disable defenses and blind intelligence capabilities in preparation for a devastating kinetic strike. These methods can slow the reactions of defenders by clouding their operation picture or fouling their communications means. Cyber attacks could bring down key command and control nodes altogether, paralyzing any response to the attack.

If the attacker has used weapons of mass destruction (chemical, biological, radiological, nuclear, and high-yield explosives) in the kinetic part of the attack, the cyber component can also hinder the ability to rally consequence-management assets. The victim will have suffered a catastrophic attack and will be unable to respond effectively to the results. The continued cyber intrusions will not only keep them from striking back with any real effect, but may make them ineffectual in mobilizing their first-responder forces.

This kind of large-scale attack can only come from a nation-state and obviously constitutes our most dangerous scenario. It is very fortunate that it is also not a very likely one.

The reason is old-fashioned deterrence. In the same way our cyber and physical infrastructures make us vulnerable to this scenario, any attacking nation-state must have its own infrastructure capabilities to be able to execute it. Those cyber capabilities and kinetic forces used in the attack are also potential targets, as is the remainder of the attacker's critical infrastructure.

Basically, it is unlikely that a nation-state would do this, because they also have much at stake. Deterrence, in the same way we have understood it for over 50 years, still applies to nation-states in all the ways it does not apply to terrorists, criminals, and other non-state actors.

A large-scale cyber attack or cyber-enabled kinetic attack by a peer competitor on another country runs the risk of a large-scale response from the target or the target's allies and friends. While this will not dissuade every nation-state-backed cyber threat—the thousands of probes, minor attacks, and espionage actions prove that—it has continued and will continue to keep this type of nightmare scenario from moving into the "likely" category. Yes, we must prepare for it, but if this is the only thing we prepare for, we will have failed our countries.

One final thought on this subject: Opinion leaders might point to the situations in Estonia and Georgia mentioned earlier as evidence that deterrence did not work in 2007 and 2008. Friendly nations must explicitly state their intentions to protect and support one another from this sort of attack in the same way we did during the Cold War; without a strong declaratory policy of mutual defense in cyber situations, there will be no deterrence.

If we fail in this, smaller nations will continue to be at risk from larger, more powerful neighbors, and this is unacceptable. If we act strongly and in a united fashion, this will constrain nation-states—but will not constrain terrorists.

Terrorist Use of the Cyber Realm: From Small Beginnings...

It is fortunate that so far, the major terrorist organizations such as al-Qaeda and its franchises have not yet learned to fully exploit the "opportunities" in the cyber realm. We would be foolish to assume this state of affairs will persist.

Terrorists are limited in their understanding of the potential for this medium. They do use it extensively, but not for offensive actions. Most intelligence and law enforcement agencies agree that they are limited to such areas as communications, propaganda, financial dealings (fund-raising and fund transfers), recruitment, and intelligence. There is some potential use for operational planning and reconnaissance, but it is unconfirmed.

Communications security on the Internet is very attractive to terrorists. The anonymity and difficulty of tracing interactions in restricted, password-protected chat rooms and the use of encrypted e-mails give terrorists a much greater degree of operational security than other means of communications. This will continue to be a major activity for terrorists over cyber channels.

Clearly, the terrorists are very good and getting better at using the Internet for propaganda and fund-raising purposes. The increasing sophistication of their messaging shows an understanding of the potential of the cyber medium in this area. They are reaching ever-increasing audiences. YouTube-like videos of terror attacks feed the fervor of the faithful around the world and make them feel a part of the struggle. Messaging over the Internet from the leadership keeps them prominent in the minds of the mass audience and makes the most isolated spokesperson seem relevant.

These same channels are superb for fund-raising among the dispersed peoples around the world. The reach and timeliness cannot be matched by other communications means and greatly aids in their fund-raising efforts. These same characteristics apply to their recruitment programs, and the process of radicalizing individuals no longer has to take place in person, but can be greatly enhanced by cyber communication and teaching.

There are many very effective applications available that aid in basic intelligence gathering. Google Earth and similar programs can be obtained for free and will give street-view photos of potential targets, as well as excellent route and obstacle information. The tendency of most Western countries to post nearly everything there is to know about critical infrastructures on unsecured Web sites is a great boon to the terrorists and requires no more expertise than an ability to use rudimentary search engines that small children have mastered. All of this "research capability" assists the terrorists in making their standard operation procedures much easier and safer to polish to a high degree.

A new wrinkle that is developing is the use of virtual worlds. There is hard evidence of money transfers having been made within these worlds. This is done by using real cash to buy virtual currency, conducting various transactions within the virtual environment, and then converting it back into real cash again in a completely different temporal location. It is all safe, clean, legal, and nearly impossible to trace.

These virtual worlds also allow for meetings to occur in cyber space that are even more deeply covered and protected than secure chat rooms. The avatars used in virtual worlds are very difficult to identify, and rules for interaction online allow for secret activities that further shield those with much to hide.

An advanced application which has been discussed by intelligence and law enforcement agencies is the use of virtual worlds to train and rehearse for operations in the real world. This is clearly possible, but no hard evidence is yet available to prove that terrorists are now using the virtual worlds in this way.

Someone must lead the terrorists of the world to the next level of cyber capability. It is unlikely that they will develop their own cyber plans and abilities beyond a few experts to ensure they are not being cheated or who can do operational cyber planning correctly. To do more than that would take a great deal of time, and they may be unwilling to wait. Unfortunately, they do not need to wait, as they will probably do it by reaching out to the world of cyber crime. There they will find willing partners.

Cyber Crime: Follow the Money

Cyber crime continues to be a booming business. What started as an offshoot of individual hackers doing it for fun and pride has grown into a huge (and still expanding) industry that steals, cheats, and extorts the equivalent of many billions of dollars every year. They steal from individuals, corporations, and countries. It does not matter if it is simple scams to get gullible people to give up money and access to their accounts or highly sophisticated technical methods of harvesting mass amounts of personal data that can be exploited directly or sold to others; cyber crime is big money. The more sophisticated it gets, the more organized it becomes, and it has matured to a frightening level.

A lucrative target is data well beyond personal identity and financial information. Infiltrating businesses and stealing industrial secrets, pharmaceutical formulas, and like data can reap huge profits for criminals.

There are several reports of utility facilities having their SCADA (supervisory control and data acquisition) systems hacked and seized by criminals. The attackers have threatened to shut down the facility or worse if they were not paid enormous ransoms. No one knows if the malefactors could have actually followed through on the shutdown threats, as in each case the money was paid. The owners deemed it a credible threat and could not afford to have their enterprise closed or destroyed.

An interesting addition to this issue set is the illegal or quasi-legal franchising of cyber crime. Criminals now market and sell the tools of cyber crime. Root kits, hacking lessons, guides to designing malware—it is all available. These range from rudimentary "starter kits" to highly sophisticated programs that are potentially very destructive.

The last and, in my mind, most interesting and insidious threat is the rise of the botnets. Criminals cannot command entire nations of computers as one would expect that coercive governments could if they need to. Criminal syndicates have, however, developed huge botnets with members all over the world: members that they control without the actual owner of the machine even being aware of it. These zombie networks serve their criminal masters without question or hesitation. The criminals control them completely and can use them directly for DDoS (distributed denial of service) attacks, phishing, or malware distribution. They also rent them out to others for cash.

An anecdote will illustrate how pervasive this is. During an industry association meeting held in December of 2008, a US Department of Homeland Security (DHS) official involved in cyber security related an incident that had occurred a few days prior. He said he had been meeting with a group of business leaders, and they expressed concern about a holiday season trend they had noticed. They complained that every year many young people received new computers as gifts, causing a big spike in computer intrusions. They blamed this on the young people using the new devices to try and hack government and business systems.

The DHS official explained to the leaders that they were only half right. He went on to explain that the many new machines were connected to the spike in intrusions—however, not because their owners were all would-be hackers. The problem lay in the fact that in some cases, within 10 to 15 minutes of a new computer being hooked to the Internet, it was infected by malware and added to a criminal botnet. The longest an unprotected or underprotected computer would last was a day or two. It was criminal-controlled botnets that were behind the spike in intrusions. They simply had many new machines to utilize in their activities.

It is here that a new and very dangerous potential arises.

Terrorism Enabled by Cyber Criminals: Most Likely Cyber Threat

There is no doubt that terrorists want badly to hurt the modern Western and Western-leaning community of nations. The numerous dead and wounded, the horrific damage of past successful attacks, as well as the multiple foiled plots all make the deadly intent of the terrorists abundantly clear to all. This cannot be denied. Their continuing efforts to acquire and develop weapons of mass destruction for use against civilian targets is also prima facie evidence of this burning desire to do us harm in any way possible.

Terrorist organizations surely can find a number of highly trained, intelligent, and computer-literate people who are in agreement with their cause. These people can be taught to develop code, write malware, and hack as well as anyone. They cannot, in a timely manner, develop the kind of large-scale operational capabilities that a nation-state possesses. This is what they need to make a truly effective assault on the West in the cyber realm.

Two factors give them another option. First, they do not really need to attack an entire nation to achieve success. They desire to create a large event, but it does not necessarily need to be as extensive as a full nation-state attack. The second factor is that they also have abundant funds and potential access to even more. These funds open up the criminal option, which will give the terrorists the capability to be extraordinarily destructive.

The West has a huge number of intelligence and law enforcement assets dedicated to stopping the proliferation of weapons of mass destruction. Any movement of these devices or materials related to them will sound the alarm across the world. Numerous arrests of people attempting to traffic in WMD or related materials have been made. This effort has nullified the effect of the excellent financial assets some terrorists have and frustrated their efforts to acquire WMD capabilities. We do not have the same type of watchdog systems in place to prevent cyber enablement from occurring.

If a cash-rich terrorist group would use its wealth to hire cyber criminal botnets for their own use, we would have a major problem. A terrorist group so enabled could begin to overwhelm the cyber defenses of a specific corporation, government organization, or infrastructure sector and do much damage. They could destroy or corrupt vital data in the financial sector, cripple communications over a wide area to spread panic and uncertainty.

Similar to the nation-state attack scenarios discussed earlier, terrorists could use botnet-driven DDoS attacks to blind security forces at a border crossing point as a means of facilitating an infiltration operation, or a cyber attack in one area of a country to act as a diversion so a "conventional" kinetic terrorist attack can occur elsewhere. They could even conduct SCADA attacks on specific sites and use the system to create kinetic-like effects without the kinetic component. A good example would be to open the valves at a chemical plant near a population center, creating a Bhopal-like event.

The permutations are as endless as one's imagination. The cyber capabilities that the criminals could provide would in short order make any terrorist organization infinitely more dangerous and effective.

Some have opined that cyber attacks are not suitable as terror tactics because they lack the drama and spectacular effect of, say, a suicide bomber. This does not take into account the ability of the terrorists to adapt. As our intelligence and law enforcement agencies continue to effectively combat the terrorists, they will continue to evolve. The terrorists' old methods will be augmented and improved. They will need to develop more imagination and versatility if they are to conduct successful operations.

This evolutionary capability has not been in short supply among the terrorist leadership. They will not define "spectacular" so narrowly. Imagine the operational elegance of simply hitting the return key and seeing thousands of enemies die a continent away, or watching a bank go under due to the destruction of all its data by an unknown force. This will be enormously attractive to terrorist groups. Additionally, the combination of cyber methods and kinetic strikes could be spectacular regardless of one's definition.

Criminals, for their part, are motivated by greed and power. Few of the leaders of the enormous cyber organized crime world would hesitate at selling their capabilities to a terrorist loaded with cash. That fact, combined with the ever-growing terrorist awareness of cyber vulnerabilities, makes this set of scenarios not just likely, but nearly inevitable.

Conclusion

Terrorists will recognize the opportunity the cyber world offers sooner or later. They will also recognize that they need help to properly exploit it. It is unlikely they will have the patience to develop their own completely independent capabilities. At the same time, the highly developed, highly capable cyber criminal networks want money and care little about the source.

This is a marriage made in Hell. The threat of a full nation-state attack, either cyber or cyber-enabled kinetic, is our most dangerous threat. We pray deterrence will continue to hold, and we should take all measures to shore up that deterrence.

Terrorists will never be deterred in this way. They will continue to seek ways to successfully harm us, and they will join hands with criminal elements to do so. A terrorist attack enabled by cyber crime capabilities will now be an eighth group of cyber threats, and it will be the most likely major event we will need to confront.

Some would say that cyber crime is a purely law enforcement issue, with no national security component. That is a dubious "truth" today. This is not a static situation, and it will definitely be more dangerously false in the future. Unless we get cyber crime under control, it will mutate into a very real, very dangerous national security issue with potentially catastrophic ramifications. It would be far better to address it now rather than in the midst of a terrorist incident or campaign of incidents against one of our countries.

Terrorism enabled by cyber criminals is our most likely major cyber threat. It must be met with all our assets.

Cyberterrorism Is a Looming Threat

Sebastian J. Bae

In the following viewpoint, Sebastian J. Bae argues that the internet has become a new breeding ground for criminals and terrorists. He covers a number of potentially dire consequences of modern society's reliance on a digital economy. Nevertheless, Bae does not believe a doomsday attack on countries or their economies is currently imminent or possible. He still believes in vigilance, but also warns that someone must keep those who are watching internet activity from abusing their powers. Sebastian J. Bae served six years in the Marine Corps infantry. He is currently an international security analyst and writes for periodicals such as Foreign Policy.

As you read, consider the following questions:

1. How does Bae define "cyberterrorism"?
2. What "apocalyptic" or "doomsday" cyberterrorist attacks does the article discuss?
3. Why does Bae believe that a single cyberterrorist attack cannot bring down a country or an economy?

Recently, there have been no shortage of cyber security headlines. In their July 12th issue, *The Economist* presented a special briefing on cyber security. Eye-catching titles like "Hackers Inc" and "Defending the Digital Frontier" painted the Internet as the new wild, wild West—rampant with virus slinging hackers. Similarly,

"Cyber-Terrorism: Fact or Fiction?" by Sebastian J. Bae, International Affairs Forum, November 22, 2017. Reprinted by Permission.

on July 10th, the cover story of *Time* magazine was "World War Z: How Hackers Fight to Steal Your Secrets." Compounded by the seemingly endless revelations of electronic surveillance and misconduct of the NSA by Edward Snowden, cyber security has become the new hot button topic. However, among the chatter and fear mongering of hackers and cyber wars between states, where does cyber-terrorism fit in the new digital world of rising threats?

Since the Global War on Terror, cyber-terrorism has become the new encompassing threat. In 2008, the World Cyber Security Summit or WCSS gathered in Malaysia to discuss future steps against the potential disastrous consequences of cyber intrusions. The meeting represented "the largest ministerial-level gathering ever organized about cyber-terrorism" drawing representatives from all over the world (Salek, 2008). Meanwhile, mainstream media has warned the public of doomsday scenarios where terrorists hijack critical infrastructures like the water supply and electrical grid with deadly consequences. Consequently, cyber-terrorism has become the new obsession of the security community as cyber-security centres have emerged one after another. The United States like many other Western states has established various cyber-security orientated agencies like newly established US Cyber Command to combat the threat of cyber-terrorism and cyberwar. Meanwhile, existing agencies like the FBI, CIA, and NSA have expanded their purviews into the cyber realm as well. Reacting to the new digital threat of terrorism, the International Multilateral Partnership Against Cyber-Terrorism or IMPACT has even boldly announced, "cyber-terrorism is real" (Salek, 2008). However, the line between cyber criminals and cyber terrorist is a slippery slope. For years, academics and policy makers alike have spilled an ocean of ink over the definition of terrorism and who qualifies as an terrorist—and there still is no definitive answer. Thus, we must begin with the basics: Does cyber-terrorism even exist?

For the confines of this essay, cyber-terrorism is "the pre-meditated, politically motivated attack against information, computer systems, computer programs, and data which results in violence against non-combatant targets by subnational groups or clandestine agents" (Verton, 2003, 27). The definition does not restrict cyber-terrorism to the narrow confines of cyber space. For instance, a computer virus or an explosive device targeting critical computer systems are both equally acts of cyber-terrorism within this context. The wider definitional berth is given due to the multi-faceted nature of terrorist operations—involving multiple tactics and tools simultaneously. In essence, cyber-terrorism can be understood as the convergence of virtual space and politics of terrorism. Within cyber-terrorism, the capability of computers and the reach of the Internet supplement or replace the traditional methods of physical damage through explosives and small arms (Weimann, 2006, 154).

The vulnerabilities in cyber security are significant, and should not be underestimated. Maintaining security in the constantly evolving digital age remains a daunting challenge. Physical society and the digital world are colliding and converging at a frightening speed from smart houses to our dependence on automation. However, the hysteria surrounding cyber-terrorism is more myth than reality. The hyper-securitized post-9/11 world has found imagined enemies everywhere including cyber space. For the moment, cyber-terrorism remains more a product of our own fears and imaginations than rooted in reality. In the end, the threat of cyber-attacks is very real, but the reality of cyber-terrorism has not yet materialized.

Vulnerable, But Not Doomed

In the modern era, interconnectedness and interdependency of systems has become a given, a fact of life. For instance, electrical grids are largely computerized which support sectors ranging from commercial banking to first responders. Technology has become the bloodline of modern states. The danger of cyber-terrorism lies in underestimating our "overwhelming dependency upon IT-related resources to continue business operations and execute recovery plans" (Verton, 2003, 23). The fear of cyber-terrorism

Cyberterrorism Is a Product of the Information Age

As the world enters the 21st century, the information revolution will continue to propel the United States into the "third wave" of development according to Alvin and Heidi Toffler. The shift from an industrial economy and society to one focused on information and its transfer will characterize the third wave. As discussed in *The Third Wave* and their most recent work, *War and Anti-War*, the way a state wages war is similar to how it makes wealth. This idea might be applied to terrorism and revolutionary violence.

Lewis Gann's *Guerrillasin History* provides an overview of substate violence across history. Occasionally, as in the Welsh use of the longbow, substate groups possess weapons superior to those of the state. Substate actors, unless being supplied by another state, normally possess weapons that are inferior to those of the target state, They often use weapons stolen from, or discarded by, the state. As the technology, complexity, and lethality of weapons systems increased during the twentieth century, these weapons were even more tightly controlled by the state, widening the gap between state and substate " firepower." As the world shifts into the information age, this disparity in weapons decreases, with individuals and substate groups now able to control information manipulation tools that were once restricted to the state.

As the world shifts into the "third wave," where information and its control are rapidly becoming *the* most important considerations for the advancing societies of the first world, will we see a corresponding shift by terrorists and revolutionaries to using "information warfare" weapons and techniques to press their case? While terrorists and revolutionaries have "kept pace with the advance of technology, consistently exploiting new and under defended targets, (embassies, airplane hijackings, hostage taking, airplane bombing) they have done so through evolution, not innovation. Bruce Hoffman contends, "What innovation does occur is mostly in the methods used to conceal and detonate explosive devise, not in their tactics or in their use of non-conventional weapons (i.e., chemical, biological, or nuclear)." ... There has already been a shift toward "information warfare" across other parts of the "conflict spectrum" with these techniques being used by criminals, agents of espionage, revolutionaries, and armies engaged in warfare.

"Information Age Terrorism: Toward Cyberterror," by Matthew J. Littleton, Federation of American Scientists, December 1995.

exists in the potential ability of a terrorist group to obtain access to critical infrastructure systems with devastating consequences. For instance, trillions of dollars rely on electronic transactions and payment systems on a daily basis. Hence, a terrorist organization could potentially create an electrical blackout with subsequent denial of services of key industries, throwing a digital economy into turmoil. A national economy could potentially be crippled instantaneously with millions lost in moments (Verton, 2003, 47-48). These scenarios represent the core fears rooted in cyber-terrorism, a combination of the fear of terrorism and the pervasiveness of technology.

Although such apocalyptic scenarios are unlikely, computerized systems do inherently have three key risk factors—access, integrity, and confidentiality. Computer systems fundamentally depend on the system's ability to access information and programs to operate. Networking various systems together has enabled greater speed and productivity. At the same time, networking computer systems together has inherently increased the collective vulnerability. Computerized systems must remain accessible to proper authorities, while maintaining system integrity from outside forces simultaneously (Pollitt, 1998, 9). The demand to balance free flowing information and cutting-edge speed, while maintaining secure servers remains a constant challenge. According to recent studies, "power and energy companies averaged 12.5 severe or critical attacks requiring immediate intervention per company" (Verton, 2003, 39). The cyber incursions reflect the dynamic nature of cyber space, constantly demanding attention and adaptation to new threats. Thus, many pundits of the cyber-terrorism threat camp argue supervisory control and data acquisitions systems or SCADA systems inherently possess vulnerabilities to cyber-terrorism. SCADA systems control a myriad of critical infrastructure systems ranging from nuclear plants, water supplies, and the electrical grid. Many argue that a determined enemy could gain access and orchestrate devastating consequences ranging from flooding communities through dams or instigate rolling blackouts. Although companies claim their security measures are sufficient, critics like Dan Verton argues, "If you talk to state and local governments and local utilities, they'll tell you they have great response plans. The problem is, they write them in isolation" (Verton, 2003, 20). The challenge is not whether one company is secure or not, but whether the entire network of individual companies and systems remains secure.

Computer vulnerabilities remain a grim reality of digital age. In April 2014, security researches announced a critical security flaw known as the Heartbleed bug in the popular data encryption standard, OpenSSL. The Heartbleed bug is the unforeseen vulnerability in the system's verification method. In OpenSSL, a computer will send a "heartbeat" or a small packet of data to verify another computer is on the other end of the secure line. However, the Heartbleed bug reveals a systemic vulnerability where hackers can extract massive data from servers, which are supposedly "secure," by creating a false "heartbeat" (Russell, 2014). In essence, the Heartbleed bug renders the popular encryption program critically fallible. According to a recent survey, "959,000,000 websites, 66% of sites are powered by technology built around SSL" are vulnerable (Russell, 2014). Thus, the Heartbleed bug, the latest cyber threat, demonstrates cyber vulnerability is not a myth, but very real. At the same time, cyber-attacks "against the Internet increase at an annual rate above 60% (Weimann, 2006, 153). The ever-increasing number of attacks reflects both the vulnerabilities of computer systems, but also the decreasing skill gap among states and sub-state actors. As with any new technology, "the cost and other barriers to developing an advanced cyber offensive are declining each year" (Knake, 2010).

Similarly, the public sector remains equally vulnerable to cyber-attacks. In 1997, the US Joint Chiefs of Staff organized an exercise to assess the Pentagon's ability to defend against a coordinated cyber incursion code named Eligible Receiver. The operational NSA Red Team were allowed to use any software freely available on the Internet, but were not allowed to break any laws. During the exercise, the NSA Red Team effectively mapped Pentagon networks, acquired passwords, created false administrator accounts, and gained almost unfettered access to particular servers (Verton, 2003, 31-33). The operation proved far more successful than any of the Joint Chiefs imagined possible. Nonetheless, Eligible Receiver provides a poignant reflection of the current cyber-terrorism landscape—one of concrete vulnerability and imagined threat. The operation doubtlessly revealed gaps in security at the Pentagon in regards to cyber threats. However, at the same time, the NSA Red Team was comprised of elites in the computer science field who had intimate knowledge of the government systems. The collective operational skills of the NSA Red Team arguably surpass most terrorist organizations. The inherent technical bias of the operators playing the Red Team adds a dimension of skepticism to the ability of terrorists to gain the same level of access.

However, there is no doubt vulnerabilities will only increase "as societies move to a ubiquitous computing environment" where more daily activities rely on remote computer automation (Lewis, 2002, 11). However, complete security is a myth whether in the physical world or in cyber space. Vulnerabilities will always exist, as total security often is synonymous with complete isolation. Thus, within a society where information and goods can move relatively freely, impregnable security is an unachievable standard. Vulnerability does not necessarily equate to disaster. For instance, banks are far from impregnable, as the history of bank robberies has clearly demonstrated. Nevertheless, despite their continual vulnerability, banks continue to adapt and function as an integral aspect of the economy. Similarly, computer systems may possess vulnerabilities that require constant evolution, but it does not doom a society to a "Digital Pearl Harbour." The 1998 attack by the Internet Black Tigers, a branch of the LTTE, remains the closest act to cyber-terrorism ever recorded. The Internet Black Tigers initiated an email bombardment of the Sri Lankan embassies creating a temporary denial-of-service (Denning, 2001, 281). However, the coordinated denial-of-service operation is far from the "doomsday scenarios" often perpetuated in the security community. Moreover, the cyber-attack by the LTTE barely compares to their deadly campaigns of suicide bombings in 1990 against Indian peacekeeping forces in Sri Lanka (Pedahzur, 2005, 76–77). Ultimately, vulnerability does not necessarily equate to disaster.

The Imagined Spectre of Cyber-terrorism

Terrorist organizations have turned to the Internet as a powerful tool in regards to logistics, propaganda, and communication. For instance, Hezbollah independently operates three different website domains for specific purposes—one for the central press office, one dedicated to attacks on Israel, and one for news and information (Denning, 2001, 252). Furthermore, a 1998 report by *US News & World Report* indicated 12 of the 30 groups on the US State Department terrorist list were featured on the Internet (Denning, 2001, 252). The number has only increased since the advent of the Global War of Terror and the rise of radical Islam. The Internet has become a digital frontier where militias, freedom fighters, mercenaries, propagandists, and terrorists find both refuge and support. However, the use of computers and technology by terrorist organizations "as facilitators of activities, whether for propaganda, communication, or other purposes is simply that: use"—not cyber-terrorism (Weimann, 2006, 154). For instance, the use of computers to create travel plans, communicate, and purchase tickets by a group of terrorists in Delray Beach, Florida, in 2001, does not constitute cyber-terrorism, merely use (Gordon & Ford, 2002, 637). For the moment, terrorist organizations have not ventured into the realm of cyber-terrorism.

Despite theories and rampant fears surrounding cyber-terrorism, "interest does not equal capability" (Knake, 2010). Although cyber-terrorism holds destructive potential, the ability to execute a complicated and deadly cyber-attack requires a sophisticated knowledge and skill set. In 2007, a research survey indicated roughly 48.5% of a sample of 404 members of violent Islamist groups possessed higher education (Conway, 2011, 27). The study disproves the popular notion that most terrorists are uneducated fanatics of the developing world. However, the study also concluded "less than 2% of the jihadis came from a computing background" (Conway, 2011, 28). Furthermore, merely possessing a computing background does not necessarily translate to the technical ability to execute a complex cyber-attack. The Centre for the Study of Terrorism and Irregular Warfare at the Naval Postgraduate School (NPS) reported, "terrorists generally lack the wherewithal and human capital needed to mount attacks that involve more than annoying but relatively harmless hacks" (Weimann, 2004, 10). Essentially, terrorist organizations have not nurtured or acquired the capability to match their interest in cyber-terrorism.

In 2002, the US government hosted a joint war exercise, code named Digital Pearl Harbour, to further assess the validity of doomsday cyber-terrorism scenarios. The results of the war exercise were far from the widespread fears surrounding cyber-terrorism. Although the opposition was able to cause sporadic damage, their primary objective to crash the Internet failed. The subsequent report by CNet concluded that a high profile cyber terrorist attack "would require a syndicate with significant resources, including $200 million, country-level intelligence and five years of preparation time" (Weimann, 2004, 10). The exercise demonstrated vulnerabilities could potentially be exploited to cause temporary disruptions. The prevalence of cybercrime and hackers has clearly demonstrated the potential for criminal elements to exploit weaknesses for personal or political motives. However, the crippling cyber-terrorism of our imaginations was abruptly debunked by operation Digital Pearl Harbour. Despite the political paranoia, "no single instance of cyber-terrorism has yet been recorded" (Weimann, 2006, 149). The fact remains the threat of cyber-terrorism has not yet truly materialized. According to the Centre of Strategic & International Studies, "electronic intrusion represents an emerging, but still relatively minor threat" (Lewis, 2002, 5). Terrorists have not joined the ranks of hackers, activists, and cyber criminals who comprise the large majority of cyber-attacks.

Since 9/11, discourses in security and terrorism have become a mixture of politics, reality, and fear mongering. As a result, statistics and research have often been skewed and manipulated to fit within particular political agendas of individuals and administrations. For instance, in December 2001, the Potomac Institute, a think tank with intimate ties with the Pentagon, announced the existence of an "Iraq Net." According to the think tank, Iraq established a network of over one hundred websites globally to launch denial-of-services or DoS attacks against American companies. However, similar to reports of weapons of mass destruction in Iraq, the Iraq Net has proven to be more fiction than truth (Weimann, 2004, 3). Similarly, cyber-terrorism has become the new galvanizing term in the Global War on Terror—attracting both funding and influence. Since the 9/11 attacks, the US government has dedicated roughly $4.5 billion USD to infrastructure protection, while the FBI "boasts more than one thousand cyber-investigators" (Weimann, 2005, 134). Thus, the domestic dimension of cyber-terrorism cannot be ignored in the perpetuation of the fear mongering plaguing cyber-terrorism. Jim Harper, director of information policy studies at the CATO Institute, states, "we're convincing ourselves that cyberspace is an endless sea of vulnerabilities that leave us weak and exposed. It's not" ("The Underwhelming," 2011). The perceived threat of cyber-terrorism has created an entire industry, both public and private. From IT companies to intelligence agencies, cyber-terrorism has launched a flurry of new cyber security centres and programs. Director Harper adeptly states, "cyber-terrorism is 'cyber–snake oil'" ("The Underwhelming," 2011). Tragically, the snake oil of cyber-terrorism does not come cheap.

Additionally, there exist doubts on the assumed success of a singular cyber-attack by terrorist organizations. During WWII, strategic bombing had entered the war's arsenal with unfettered restraint. Similar to cyber-terrorism, strategic bombing targeted critical infrastructure to destroy the enemy's ability in regards to economic and military production with the added dimension of social fear. The parallels between strategic bombing and cyberterrorism are striking. Allied Forces bombarded entire cities including Berlin, Dresden, and Tokyo. Regardless of one's moral judgment on the merits of strategic bombing, the Strategic Bombing Survey concluded, "The German experience showed that, whatever the target system, no indispensable industry was permanently put out of commission by a single attack. Persistent re-attack was necessary" (Lewis, 2002, 3). Thus, strategic bombing provides a critical insight into the nature of cyber-terrorism. A singular act of cyber-terrorism will not destroy a nation or an economy. Like strategic bombing, truly effective cyber-terrorism will require persistent, unrelenting cyber incursions to fully cripple a nation. In essence, "the sky is not falling, and cyber weapons seem to be of limited value in attacking national power or intimidating citizens" (Lewis, 2002, 10).

Furthermore, unlike physical attacks, cyber operations introduce new operational challenges to terrorist organizations. Computer systems are complex and involve a high level of operational coordination and control. Nurturing new innovative skills sets prove challenging for any organization including terrorist groups. The capacity building around cyber-terrorism has stalled similar to maritime terrorism. At the moment, the current generation of terrorist organization lacks the technical prowess for cyber-terrorism. However, this may not always be the case. Frank Cilluffo, the Associate Vice President for Homeland Security at George Washington University, warned, "While bin Laden may have his finger on the trigger, his grandchildren may have their fingers on the computer mouse" (Weimann, 2005, 146). Terrorist organizations like al-Qaeda have proven themselves to be startlingly innovative and adaptive. Nevertheless, even a successful cyber-attack upon critical infrastructure may not conjure the same level of trauma, drama, and damage as traditional terrorist methods (Denning, 2001, 282). For instance, when Enron and El Paso Corps orchestrated power outages and rolling blackouts through California in 2002, there was no cataclysmic fallout in death and destruction (Thurm, Gavin, & Benson, 2002). The blackouts affected the 32 million residents of California and virtually stalled its 32 trillion dollar economy overnight—similar to the feared consequences of cyber-terrorism. However, the incident did not embody the panic of any Digital Pearl Harbour scenario, but demonstrated the resiliency of critical infrastructure to recover relatively quickly. In the end, the fact remains "no human death has been clearly linked to cyber-attacks whether they were terrorism or criminal act" (Gorge, 2007, 12).

Conclusion

James Lewis of the Centre for Strategic and International Security emphatically stated, "Digital Pearl Harbours are unlikely" (Lewis, 2002, 11). The fact remains the cyber-terrorism touted in official reports and mainstream media has not materialized. For the moment, cyber-terrorism remains more a product of fear and imagination than concrete reality. Nonetheless, in the new globalized digital world, the lines between foreign and domestic, private and public, and the virtual and physical worlds are rapidly blurring. Similarly, security challenges are progressively growing amorphous—actions in cyber space possess growing physical consequences. Yet currently, the threat of cyber-terrorism remains largely exaggerated. Nevertheless, the potential cannot be completely ignored either. As the world becomes more intertwined with the digital world, cyber-terrorism may not remain a ghost of our fears, but a stark reality of the times. Terrorist organizations have proven to innovative, unconventional, and wholly determined. Hence, we must equally be innovative and adaptive, while maintaining our clarity of thought and resisting the easy answers of fear mongering. Yet for the moment, states and policy makers have a more pressing issues concerning cyber security—the foremost being the precarious balance between cyber security and personal privacy. Before we can tackle the invisible enemies beyond our walls we must make sure we do not allow the guards to become the threat from within. Who will watch the watchers? Who reads their emails?

Viewpoint 3

ISIS's Current Digital Capabilities Are Limited, But Not Harmless

Audie Cornish and Mary Louise Kelly

In the following viewpoint, an interview on National Public Radio (NPR), hosts Audie Cornish and Mary Louise Kelly discuss the potential of one terrorist group, the Islamic State of Iraq and Syria (ISIS), to attack countries such as the United States through cyberterrorism. ISIS's chief online strategy has been pushing propaganda and recruitment through social media, but the group, dedicated to inflicting pain by any means possible, has sought to expand its digital terror capabilities as well. Despite this uncomfortable notion, ISIS is not thought to be capable of perpetration a cyber 9/11. Audie Cornish and Mary Louise Kelly co-host NPR's All Things Considered. Kelly was previously a national security correspondent for NPR.

As you read, consider the following questions:

1. What are ISIS's capabilities in the area of social media, defensive digital weaponry, and offensive digital weaponry?
2. Why are ISIS's current online offensive capabilities referred to as only "pinpricks"?
3. In what manner did ISIS actually hack into the United States military and was this hacking significant?

The US and the West aren't the only ones operating on the cyber-battlefield in the war with ISIS. The terror group has cyber-capabilities of its own. NPR takes a look at these capabilities and explores how they play into the larger expansion of cyber-strike and counter-strike throughout the Middle East.

AUDIE CORNISH, HOST: In Hannover, Germany today, President Obama had this to say about ISIS.

BARACK OBAMA: These terrorists are doing everything in their power to strike our cities and kill our citizens, so we need to do everything in our power to stop them.

CORNISH: Everything in our power includes using cyber weapons. NPR's Mary Louise Kelly has recently reported on how the US is stepping up cyberattacks against ISIS, so we asked her to consider the flip side, how ISIS is trying to attack the US online. Mary Louise, welcome to the studio.

MARY LOUISE KELLY, BYLINE: Nice to be here, Audie.

CORNISH: Let's start there. Can you give us the big picture in terms of capabilities—right?—for ISIS? How adept are they at using, I guess, online tools as a weapon?

KELLY: Sure. And let me try to frame it by breaking it into three prongs. One, we know—we have seen they are very good at using social media to recruit, to spread their message. Two, we know that they are very good at using cyber as a defensive weapon. We saw that with the Paris attacks, with the Brussels attacks. They were able to use encrypted communications to plan those, to carry them out without being detected.

But the third prong is their offensive capability. How good are they—or not—in using cyber as a tool of terror to be able to attack the US and the West? And that question—how good they are, what their capabilities are—that is a big question. It is a live question right now at the White House, at the Pentagon, elsewhere within the US government.

CORNISH: Well, what's known? I mean, has ISIS actually carried out a significant cyberattack to date?

KELLY: The short answer is no. And that is, of course, good news. Adm. Mike Rogers who is the head both of US Cyber Command and of the National Security Agency was asked that very question actually on Capitol Hill earlier this month. He said ISIS's ability today to use cyber as a weapon is limited. But he also said if they decide they want to carry out a cyberattack in the US, it would—and I'm quoting—not be difficult for them. And I think that gets to the question of intent, Audie.

One former Pentagon official I spoke with who's worked cyber issues, he agreed ISIS's current capability is limited. He described it as pinpricks at best. But he said consider this—what if they decide they want to buy that capability? Because we know they have money despite US efforts to disrupt their finances. There are people out there with expertise who might be persuaded to share it for the right price.

CORNISH: Any guess as to who might do so? I mean, are there names that the US Intelligence Committee is tracking?

KELLY: One key name that a lot of attention was paid to was Junaid Hussain, a British hacker—now a dead British hacker. He was killed in Syria last year in a US drone strike. He hacked US military accounts, published the names and photos of US troops online. And then he tweeted to his followers and said go try to find these people and kill them.

The two takeaways I would say—one, he didn't succeed, and two, that is—as awful as it is—that is not shutting down the US power grid, for example. That is not a US cyber 9/11. It's not even close. They are not there yet.

CORNISH: Although, we should mention—didn't ISIS hack Central Command?

KELLY: They did last year. They hacked into the CENTCOM Twitter account, and they posted an image of a masked militant. They posted the message, I love you, ISIS, so a huge embarrassment. The Pentagon was quick to point out, hey, this was a Twitter feed. This was not CENTCOM classified accounts. However, I think it drove home the point this is an asymmetric battle that cyber is a great equalizer. All you need is one guy who is determined with a laptop and the ability to write code, new world.

CORNISH: That's NPR's Mary Louise Kelly. Thank you so much.

KELLY: You're welcome.

Viewpoint 4

Cyber-Doom Scenarios Are Rooted in Fears of Technology Out of Control

Sean Lawson

In the following excerpted viewpoint, Sean Lawson discusses "cyber-doom" scenarios and the fears and potential realities associated with such world-shattering events. Many experts in cybersecurity have pondered the possibility of such scenarios, and much of our fear of such events results from a worry about technology out of control. Such anxiety concerning societal dependence on technology has a long history, but these fears usually not borne out in actual practice. Sean Lawson is Associate Professor in the Department of Communication at the University of Utah. He is author of the book, Nonlinear Science and Warfare: Chaos, Complexity, and the US Military in the Information Age.

As you read, consider the following questions:

1. Why are cyber-doom scenarios an important tactic used by cybersecurity proponents?
2. What is the history of cyberdoom scenarios?
3. Why is technology-out-of-control such a central fear among the general public and cybersecurity experts?

"Beyond Cyber-Doom: Cyberattack Scenarios and the Evidence of History," by Sean Lawson, Mercatus Center at George Mason University, January 2011. Reprinted by permission.

Despite persistent ambiguity in cyber-threat perceptions, cyber-doom scenarios have remained an important tactic used by cybersecurity proponents. Cyber-doom scenarios are hypothetical stories about prospective impacts of a cyberattack and are meant to serve as cautionary tales that focus the attention of policy makers, media, and the public on the issue of cybersecurity. These stories typically follow a set pattern involving a cyberattack disrupting or destroying critical infrastructure. Examples include attacks against the electrical grid leading to mass blackouts, attacks against the financial system leading to economic losses or complete economic collapse, attacks against the transportation system leading to planes and trains crashing, attacks against dams leading floodgates to open, or attacks against nuclear power plants leading to meltdowns (Cavelty, 2007: 2).

Recognizing that modern infrastructures are closely interlinked and interdependent, such scenarios often involve a combination of multiple critical infrastructure systems failing simultaneously, what is sometimes referred to as a "cascading failure." This was the case in the "Cyber Shockwave" war game televised by CNN in February 2010, in which a computer worm spreading among cell phones eventually led to serious disruptions of critical infrastructures (Gaylord, 2010). Even more ominously, in their recent book, Richard Clarke and Robert Knake (2010: 64–68) present a scenario in which a cyberattack variously destroys or seriously disrupts all US infrastructure in only fifteen minutes, killing thousands and wreaking unprecedented destruction on US cities.

Surprisingly, some argue that we have already had attacks at this level, but that we just have not recognized that they were occurring. For example, Amit Yoran, former head of the Department of Homeland Security's National Cyber Security Division, claims that a "cyber- 9/11" has already occurred, "but it's happened slowly so we don't see it." As evidence, he points to the 2007 cyberattacks on Estonia, as well as other incidents in which the computer systems of government agencies or contractors have been infiltrated and sensitive information stolen (Singel, 2009). Yoran is not alone in seeing the 2007 Estonia attacks as an example of the cyber-doom that awaits if we do not take cyber threats seriously. The speaker of the Estonian parliament, Ene Ergma, has said that "When I look at a nuclear explosion, and the explosion that happened in our country in May, I see the same thing" (Poulsen, 2007).

Cyber-doom scenarios are not new. As far back as 1994, futurist and best-selling author Alvin Toffler claimed that cyberattacks on the World Trade Center could be used to collapse the entire US economy. He predicted that "They [terrorists or rogue states] won't need to blow up the World Trade Center. Instead, they'll feed signals into computers from Libya or Tehran or Pyongyang and shut down the whole banking system if they want to. We know a former senior intelligence official who says, 'Give me $1 million and 20 people and I will shut down America. I could close down all the automated teller machines, the Federal Reserve, Wall Street, and most hospital and business computer systems'" (Elias, 1994).

But we have not seen anything close to the kinds of scenarios outlined by Yoran, Ergma, Toffler, and others. Terrorists did not use cyberattack against the World Trade Center; they used hijacked aircraft. And the attack of 9/11 did not lead to the long-term collapse of the US economy; we would have to wait for the impacts of years of bad mortgages for a financial meltdown. Nor did the cyberattacks on Estonia approximate what happened on 9/11 as Yoran has claimed, and certainly not nuclear warfare as Ergma has claimed. In fact, a scientist at the NATO Co-operative Cyber Defence Centre of Excellence, which was established in Tallinn, Estonia in response to the 2007 cyberattacks, has written that the immediate impacts of those attacks were "minimal" or "nonexistent," and that the "no critical services were permanently affected" (Ottis, 2010: 72).

Nonetheless, many cybersecurity proponents continue to offer up cyber-doom scenarios that not only make analogies to weapons of mass destruction (WMDs) and the terrorist attacks of 9/11, but also hold out economic, social, and even civilizational collapse as possible impacts of cyberattacks. A report from the

Hoover Institution has warned of so-called "eWMDs" (Kelly & Almann, 2008); the FBI has warned that a cyberattack could have the same impact as a "well-placed bomb" (FOXNews.com, 2010b); and official DoD documents refer to "weapons of mass disruption," implying that cyberattacks might have impacts comparable to the use of WMD (Chairman of the Joint Chiefs of Staff 2004, 2006). John Arquilla, one of the first to theorize cyberwar in the 1990s (Arquilla & Ronfeldt, 1997), has spoken of "a grave and growing capacity for crippling our tech-dependent society" and has said that a "cyber 9/11" is a matter of if, not when (Arquilla, 2009). Mike McConnell, who has claimed that we are already in an ongoing cyberwar (McConnell, 2010), has even predicted that a cyberattack could surpass the impacts of 9/11 "by an order of magnitude" (*The Atlantic*, 2010). Finally, some have even compared the impacts of prospective cyberattacks to the 2004 Indian Ocean tsunami that killed roughly a quarter million people and caused widespread physical destruction in five countries (Meyer, 2010); suggested that cyberattack could pose an "existential threat" to the United States (FOXNews.com, 2010b); and offered the possibility that cyberattack threatens not only the continued existence of the United States, but all of "global civilization" (Adhikari, 2009).

In response, critics have noted that not only has the story about who threatens what, how, and with what potential impact shifted over time, but it has done so with very little evidence provided to support the claims being made (Bendrath, 2001, 2003; Walt, 2010). Others have noted that the cyber-doom scenarios offered for years by cybersecurity proponents have yet to come to pass and question whether they are possible at all (Stohl, 2007). Some have also questioned the motives of cybersecurity proponents. Various think tanks, security firms, defense contractors, and business leaders who trumpet the problem of cyber attacks are portrayed as self-interested ideologues who promote unrealistic portrayals of cyber-threats (Greenwald, 2010).

While I am sympathetic to these arguments, in this essay I would like for a moment to assume that mass disruption or destruction of critical infrastructure systems are possible entirely through the use of cyberattack. Thus, the goal in this paper will be 1) to understand the origins of such fears, 2) to assess whether the supposed second-order effects (i.e. economic, social, or civilizational collapse) of cyberattack are realistic, and 3) to assess the policy implications of relying upon such scenarios.

Cyber-Doom and Technological Pessimism

Several scholars have asked why there is such a divergence between cyber-doom scenarios and the few incidents of actual cyberattack that we have thus far witnessed (Stohl, 2007; Weimann, 2008: 42). They have resolved the paradox, in part, by pointing to the fact that fears of cyberterrorism and cyberwar combine a number of long-standing human fears, including fear of terrorism (especially since 9/11), fear of the unknown, and fear of new technologies (Stohl, 2007; Weimann, 2008: 42; Embar-Seddon, 2002: 1034). Here I will focus on the third of these, the fear of "technology out of control" as an increasingly prominent fear held by citizens of Western, industrial societies over the last century. Concerns about cybersecurity are but the latest manifestation of this fear.

Historians of technology have written extensively about the rise of the belief in "autonomous technology" or "technological determinism" in Western societies, as well as the increasingly prominent feelings of pessimism and fear that have come along with these beliefs. While many in the nineteenth century believed that technological innovation was the key to human progress (Hughes, 2004), throughout the course of the twentieth century, many began to question both humanity's ability to control its creations, as well as the impacts of those creations. Thus, we have seen the emergence of "the belief that technology is the primary force shaping the post-modern world" (Marx, 1997: 984) but also "that somehow technology has gotten out of control and follows its own course, independent of human direction" (Winner, 1977: 13). As a result, we have also seen the emergence of an increasing sense of "technological pessimism" (Marx, 1994: 238), a sense of ambivalence towards technology in which we at once marvel at the innovations that have made modern life possible, but also "a gathering sense . . . of political impotence" and "the feeling that our collective life in society is uncontrollable" as a result of our increasing dependence upon technology (Marx, 1997: 984). Technological determinism, both optimistic and pessimistic, is found in a number of recent and influential scholarly and popular works that address the role of technological change in society. These include Manuel Castells' mostly optimistic work, which identifies information and knowledge working on themselves in a feedback loop as being the core of the new economy (Castells, 2000), and Kevin Kelly's more recent and more pessimistic work that posits definition an emergent, self-reinforcing, technology dependent society he calls the "technium" (Kelly, 2010).

The character of the technologies that are most prominent in our lives has indeed changed over the last century, from individual mechanical devices created by individual inventors to large socio-technical systems created and managed by large, geographically dispersed organizations (Marx, 1994: 241; Marx, 1997: 972–974). In the twentieth century, we came to realize that "Man now lives in and through technical creations" (Winner, 1977: 34) and to "entertain the vision of a postmodern society dominated by immense, overlapping, quasi-autonomous technological systems," in which society itself becomes "a meta-system of systems upon whose continuing ability to function our lives depend." It is no wonder that the "inevitably diminished sense of human agency" that attends this vision should lead to pessimism and fear directed at technology (Marx, 1994: 257).

That these fears are manifest in contemporary concerns about cybersecurity should not come as a surprise. Scholars have noted that our reactions to new technologies are often "mediated by older attitudes" (Marx, 1994: 239) which often include a familiar "pattern of responses to new technologies that allure [and] threaten" (Simon, 2004: 23). Many of the concerns found in contemporary cybersecurity discourse are not unique, but rather,

IOT Vulnerabilities

The recent global ransomware attack, which affected organizations around the world including Britain's National Health Service, was the first real illustration for many people of the scale and physical consequences a cyber attack might present. Criminal hackers exploited a flaw in "retired" Microsoft software, which is not routinely updated and patched for security, to infect computers with the WannaCry ransomware.

But what if devices were even more vulnerable, running with no built-in security and no opportunity to patch? This is the problem that that the so-called internet of things (IOT) presents. With an anticipated 22.5 billion devices due to be connected to the internet by 2021, the opportunity for holding these devices to ransom will present significant opportunities to criminals and will have serious consequences for providers and users of these devices.

Last year the massive Distributed Denial of Service (DDoS) attack that brought down the Dyn Domain Name System (DNS) service illustrated the vulnerability of certain platforms to attacks using the IOT. During that attack the perpetrators managed to deny access to major platforms like Twitter, Netflix and Facebook for some hours. It was made possible through harnessing poorly protected household devices such as security CCTV and baby monitors which still had the factory password programmed or no built in security.

This attack was significant and cost Dyn clients but it didn't have an impact on critical infrastructure such as hospitals and doctors' surgeries in the way this current attack has, where denying access to patient records could delay essential treatment. But the IOT has had and could have further significant physical consequences, when even the most benign of objects can be weaponized.

This week an 11-year-old boy demonstrated the vulnerability of the IOT to weaponization by hacking into the devices of an audience attending a cyber security conference to operate his teddy bear. Similarly earlier this year the German Federal Network Agency advised parents to destroy the Cayla doll because of its demonstrated vulnerability to being hacked. Smart thermostats have been demonstrated as hackable, as have cars, baby monitors and televisions.

"The Internet of Things Will Be Even More Vulnerable to Cyber Attacks," by Hannah Bryce, Chatham House, May 18, 2017.

have strong corollaries in early 20th-century concerns about society's increasing reliance upon interdependent and seemingly fragile infrastructure systems of various types, including electronic communication networks.

Early forms of electronic communication, including the radio, telegraph, and telephone, sparked fear and anxiety by government officials and the public alike that are similar to contemporary concerns about cybersecurity. The US Navy was initially reluctant to adopt the radio, in part because of concern over what today would be called "information assurance" (Douglas, 1985). The early twentieth century saw an explosion in the number of amateur radio users in the United States who could not only "listen in" on military radio traffic, but who could also broadcast on the same frequencies used by the military. Amateur broadcasts could clog the airwaves, preventing legitimate military communications, but could also be used to feed false information to ships at sea. In response, the Navy worked to have amateurs banned from the airwaves. They succeeded only in 1912 after it was reported that interference by amateur radio operators may have hampered efforts to rescue survivors of the Titanic disaster. After 1912, amateurs were limited to the shortwave area of the electromagnetic spectrum and during World War I, the US government banned amateur radio broadcast entirely (Douglas, 2007: 214–215).

Contemporary cybersecurity concerns also echo the fears and anxieties that telephone and telegraph systems caused in the early 20th century. Along with transcontinental railroad networks, these "new networks of long-distance communication," which could not be "wholly experienced or truly seen," were the first of the kind of large, complex, nation-spanning, socio-technical systems that were at the heart of the last century's increasing technological pessimism (MacDougall, 2006: 720). The new communication networks were often portrayed in popular media as constituting a new space, a separate world dominated by crime, daring, and intrigue (MacDougall, 2006: 720–721). While the new communication network "gave new powers to its users, [it] also compounded the ability of distant people and events to affect those users' lives" (MacDougall, 2006: 718). In short, it introduced the power and danger of "action at a distance—the ability to act in one place and affect the lives of people in another" (MacDougall, 2006: 721). Many worried that the combination of action at a distance and the relative anonymity offered by the new communication networks would allow people to more readily engage in immoral activities like gambling, that the networks would become tools of organized crime, and even that nefarious "wire devils" could use the telegraph to crash the entire US economy (MacDougall, 2006: 724–726). Even if particular nefarious actors could not be identified, the mere fact of a "complex interdependence of technology, agriculture, and national finance" that was difficult if not impossible to apprehend was itself enough to cause anxiety (MacDougall, 2006: 724).

As in cybersecurity discourse, these fears were reflective of a more generalized anxiety about the supposed interdependence and fragility of modern, industrial societies. This anxiety shaped the thinking of military planners on both sides of the Atlantic. Early airpower theorists in the United States and the United Kingdom had these beliefs at the heart of their plans for the use of strategic bombardment. For example, in his influential 1925 book, *Paris, or the Future of War*, B.H. Liddell Hart (1925: 41) argued that "A modern state is such a complex and interdependent fabric that it offers a target highly sensitive to a sudden and overwhelming blow from the air." He continued, "a nation's nerve-system, no longer covered by the flesh of its troops, is now laid bare to attack, and, like the human nerves, the progress of civilization has rendered it far more sensitive than in earlier and more primitive times" (Hart, 1925: 37). In the United States, Major William C. Sherman, who co-authored the 1922 Air Tactics text used to train American pilots, believed industrialization to be both a blessing and a curse and his "industrial fabric" theory of aerial bombardment started from the assumption that the "very quality of modern industry renders it vulnerable" to aerial attack (Sherman, 1926: 217–218).

Like cyberwar theorists today, airpower theorists argued that the unique vulnerabilities resulting from society's new-found dependence on interlocking webs of production, transportation, and communication systems could be exploited to cause almost instantaneous chaos, panic, and paralysis in a society (Konvitz, 1990; Biddle, 2002). But just as neither telegraph "wire devils" nor nefarious Internet hackers were the cause of the economic troubles of 1929 or 2008, so too did the predictions of quick victory from the air miss their mark.

In Ukraine NotPetya Succeeded in Disrupting Businesses

Paul Haskell-Dowland

In the following viewpoint, Paul Haskell-Dowland argues that cyberattacks seem to be increasingly complex and different enough from past attacks that no one can predict or react quickly enough to them. The malware dubbed "NotPetya" used in a 2017 cyberattack was compared to the previous ransomware known as WannaCry. But investigators soon learned there were important differences and that NotPetya was likely not ransomware at all. Months after this viewpoint was written, the CIA concluded that the Russian military was responsible for the NotPetya cyberattack in an attempt to disrupt Ukraine's finance system. Haskell-Dowland is associate dean for Computing and Security in the School of Science at Edith Cowan University in Australia.

As you read, consider the following questions:

1. Which global organizations had NotPetya hit when this viewpoint was written?
2. What is an "exploit"?
3. How did NotPetya differ from traditional encryption ransomware?

"Three Ways the 'Not Petya' Cyberattack Is More Complex Than WannaCry," by Paul Haskell-Dowland, The Conversation, June 29, 2017. https://theconversation.com/three-ways-the-notpetya-cyberattack-is-more-complex-than-wannacry-80266.

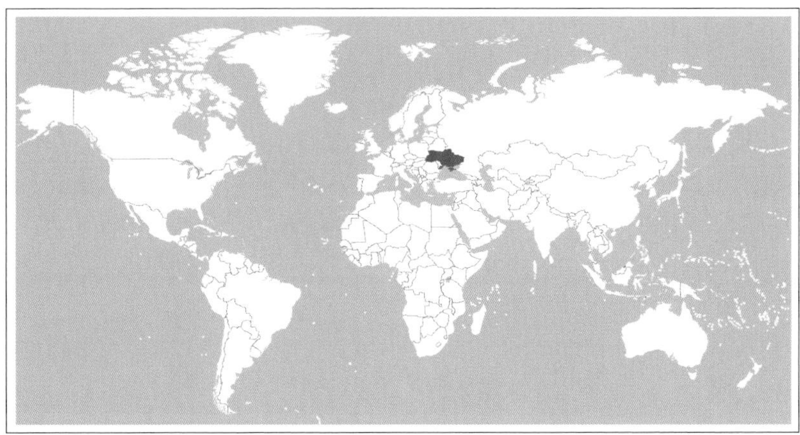

The WannaCry ransomware was barely out of the headlines when another cyberattack took down computer systems around the world.

This time, a piece of malware dubbed "NotPetya" is to blame. And unlike WannaCry, it has no clear "kill switch" as it spreads across infected networks.

NotPetya has reportedly hit several global organisations so far, including the American pharmaceutical company Merck and, in Australia, Cadbury.

The attack was initially classed as ransomware: malicious software that holds a user to ransom by encrypting their files and blocking access without a "key." It was a reasonable assumption given the threatening message displayed to victims—but the picture is more complicated.

NotPetya is distinct from WannaCry in a number of important ways—particularly, money doesn't seem to be its end goal.

1. It's about disruption not profit

Unlike other ransomware incidents, NotPetya seems to be aimed at disruption rather than criminal profiteering (or perhaps just bad design).

First, the amount requested by the ransomers is relatively small—only US$300. This seems to place a low value on the loss of access that the malware causes.

Secondly, infected machines direct the user to make payment to one Bitcoin account. Users are also referred to a single email address to obtain the keys necessary to decrypt their data. Unfortunately, many users have now discovered that the email account has been closed by Posteo, the email provider.

This means that, even having made payment for the ransom, end users are unable to recover their data. Locking yourself out from your victims with a fixed address in this manner just doesn't make good business sense.

This points either to amateurish implementation, or to the fact that NotPetya may have another purpose.

Some reports suggest the ransom demands may be a media lure to maximise public attention, while other researchers question whether recovery of encrypted data was ever possible.

In some circles, this attack has been classified as a "wiper" (in which data or even entire disks are deleted or modified beyond repair), but this is still to be firmly determined.

Whatever the case, if the perpetrators wanted to make money they have gone about it all wrong.

2. Ukraine seems to be the centre of the damage

Unlike WannaCry, which made headlines after it shut down the computer systems of British hospitals among other organisations, the largest number of NotPetya incidents have been reported in Ukraine.

The malware uses an "exploit"—a tool that can take advantage of a specific vulnerability on a computer—to remotely execute code on vulnerable Windows operating systems. This vulnerability, called MS17-010, was patched by Microsoft in March. The instances of compromised systems suggests that many organisations and individuals have failed to install the patch.

One possible explanation for high levels of non-patched systems could be the prevalence of pirated software in Ukraine.

Another distribution mechanism used by the malware appears to be a software updater linked to the Ukrainian tax accounting software, M.E.Doc.

While there is no clear evidence pointing to the perpetrators of this attack, its motivations could be political. Unlike WannaCry, NotPetya is seriously disrupting businesses rather than making money, or else is masking its other intentions.

3. It may not even be ransomware

While NotPetya uses an edited version of the same EternalBlue software exploit as the WannaCry ransomware to remotely run code on the victim's Windows computer, it differs in many key ways.

Whereas WannaCry only encrypted certain files (typically users' most important data), NotPetya also prevents access to the entire operating system. It does this by writing over key parts of the hard disk as well as encrypting users' files.

Traditional encryption ransomware typically has a key available to recover your files. With NotPetya, there is no key to facilitate recovery (despite the promises shown on screen). There is evidence that the allegedly unique ID shown to the victim is actually random data that could never result in a decryption key being provided.

While it is still too early to provide a definitive analysis of this cyberattack, it is clear this is a new twist in online warfare.

The code has been carefully designed to take advantage of vulnerable systems while the user is duped into believing that it's possible to recover their files. The ransomware distraction may have been a careful misdirection to hide the true intentions of the mayhem.

We can expect this trend to continue and that organisations (and individuals) need to be more proactive in keeping their operating systems up to date and their data backed up.

Periodical and Internet Sources Bibliography

The following articles have been selected to supplement the diverse views presented in this chapter.

WajdiHomaid Al Quliti, "The Islamic World's Response to Cyber Terrorism." *Atlantic Council*, February 8, 2017. http://www.atlanticcouncil.org/blogs/new-atlanticist/the-islamic-world-s-response-to-cyber-terrorism.

Ami Rojkes Dombe and Yoram Golandsky, "A Review and Analysis of the World of Cyber Terrorism."*Cyberisk*, April 20, 2016. https://www.cyberisk.biz/cyber-terrorism-review-and-analysis/.

Grant Gross, "UN: More international cooperation needed to fight cyberterrorism." *Computerworld*, October 24, 2012. https://www.computerworld.com/article/2492864/cybercrime-hacking/un—more-international-cooperation-needed-to-fight-cyberterrorism.html.

Keiran Hardy, "Is Cyber Terrorism a Threat?" *Australian Institute of International Affairs*, 20 Feb 2017. http://www.internationalaffairs.org.au/australianoutlook/is-cyberterrorism-a-threat/.

Ryan Littlefield, "Cyber Terrorism: understanding and preventing acts of terror within our cyber space." *Medium*, June 7, 2017. https://littlefield.co/cyber-terrorism-understanding-and-preventing-acts-of-terror-within-our-cyber-space-26ae6d53cfbb.

Ewen MacAkill, "Countries are risking cyber terrorism, security expert tells first world summit." *Guardian*, May 5, 2010. https://www.theguardian.com/technology/2010/may/05/terrorism-uksecurity.

Thomas Oriti, "Cyberterrorists targeting healthcare systems, critical infrastructure." *World Today*, October 23, 2017. http://www.abc.net.au/news/2017-10-23/forget-explosives,-terrorists-are-coming-after-cyber-systems/9076786.

Latha Subrananian, Jianhong Liu, and John Winterdyk, "Cyber-Terrorism and Cyber Security: A Global Perspective." *ResearchGate*, October 11, 2016. https://www.researchgate.net/publication/308983209_Cyber Terrorism_and_Cyber_Security_A_Global_Perspective.

Uzair M. Younus, "The Threat of Cyberterrorism." *Dawn*, March 21, 2016. https://www.dawn.com/news/1246971.

Chapter 2

State-Sponsored Cyberterrorism

Viewpoint 1

State-Sponsored Cyberattacks Are Likely to Increase

Lee Rainie, Janna Anderson, and Jennifer Connolly

In the following viewpoint, Lee Rainie, Janna Anderson, and Jennifer Connolly provide a list of the state-sponsored cyberattacks that have already occurred worldwide. They also surveyed a group of cybersecurity experts, asking each what the chances were of a major attack before 2025. The answers were varied, as would be expected, but a significant majority of the experts believed that a major attack would occur in the suggested time frame. Lee Rainie is Director of Internet and Technology at the Pew Research Center. Janna Anderson is Professor of Emerging Media and Digital Journalism at Elon University. Jennifer Connolly is Assistant Professor of Political Science at the University of Miami.

As you read, consider the following questions:

1. What examples of state-sponsored cyberattacks do the authors cite?
2. How do most of the surveyed cybersecurity experts feel about the potential for a significant cyberterrorist attack?
3. According to Jeremy Epstein, what is the primary concern when it comes to safeguarding against cyberattacks?

"Cyber Attacks Likely to Increase," by Lee Rainie, Janna Anderson, and Jennifer Connolly, Pew Research Center, October 29, 2014. Reprinted by permission.

The Internet has become so integral to economic and national life that government, business, and individual users are targets for ever-more frequent and threatening attacks.

In the 10 years since the Pew Research Center and Elon University's Imagining the Internet Center first asked experts about the future of cyber attacks in 2004 a lot has happened:

- Some suspect the Russian government of attacking or encouraging organized crime assaults on official websites in the nation of Georgia during military struggles in 2008 that resulted in a Russian invasion of Georgia.
- In 2009-2010, suspicions arose that a sophisticated government-created computer worm called "Stuxnet" was loosed in order to disable Iranian nuclear plant centrifuges that could be used for making weapons-grade enriched uranium. The *New York Times* eventually published accounts arguing that the governments of the United States and Israel designed the worm and that a programming error allowed it to be propagated around the world on the internet.
- The American Defense Department has created a Cyber Command structure that builds Internet-enabled defensive and offensive cyber strategies as an integral part of war planning and war making.
- In May, five Chinese military officials were indicted in Western Pennsylvania for computer hacking, espionage and other offenses that were aimed at six US victims, including nuclear power plants, metals and solar products industries. The indictment comes after several years of revelations that Chinese military and other agents have broken into computers at major US corporations and media companies in a bid to steal trade secrets and learn what stories journalists were working on.
- In October, Russian hackers were purportedly discovered to be exploiting a flaw in Microsoft Windows to spy on NATO, the Ukrainian government, and Western businesses.

- The respected Ponemon Institute reported in September that 43% of firms in the United States had experienced a data breach in the past year. Retail breaches, in particular, had grown in size in virulence in the previous year. One of the most chilling breaches was discovered in July at JPMorgan Chase & Co., where information from 76 million households and 7 million small businesses was compromised. Obama Administration officials have wondered if the breach was in retaliation by the Putin regime in Russia over events in Ukraine.
- Among the types of exploits of individuals in evidence today are stolen national ID numbers, pilfered passwords and payment information, erased online identities, espionage tools that record all online conversations and keystrokes, and even hacks of driverless cars.
- Days before this report was published, Apple's iCloud cloud-based data storage system was the target of a so-called "man-in-the-middle" attack in China that was aimed at stealing users' passwords and spying on their account activities. Some activists and security experts said they suspected the Chinese government had mounted the attack, perhaps because the iPhone 6 had just become available in the country. Others thought the attack was not sophisticated enough to have been government-initiated.
- The threat of cyber attacks on government agencies, businesses, non-profits, and individual users is so pervasive and worrisome that this month (October 2014) is National Cyber Security Awareness Month.

To explore the future of cyber attacks we canvassed thousands of experts and Internet builders to share their predictions. We call this a canvassing because it is not a representative, randomized survey. Its findings emerge from an "opt in" invitation to experts, many of whom play active roles in Internet evolution as technology builders, researchers, managers, policymakers, marketers, and analysts. We also invited comments from those who have made insightful predictions to our previous queries about the future of the Internet.

Overall, 1,642 respondents weighed in on the following question:

> **Major cyber attacks:** By 2025, will a major cyber attack have caused widespread harm to a nation's security and capacity to defend itself and its people? (By "widespread harm," we mean significant loss of life or property losses/damage/theft at the levels of tens of billions of dollars.)
>
> **Please elaborate on your answer.** (Begin with your name if you are willing to have your comments attributed to you.) Explain what vulnerabilities nations have to their sovereignty in the coming decade and whether major economic enterprises can or cannot thwart determined opponents. Or explain why you think the level of threat has been hyped and/or why you believe attacks can be successfully thwarted.

Some 61% of these respondents said "yes" that a major attack causing widespread harm would occur by 2025 and 39% said "no."

There was little disagreement that the spread and importance of the Internet in the lives of people, businesses, and government agencies exposes them all to new dangers.

As Jay Cross, the chief scientist at Internet Time Group, summarized his "yes" answer: "Connectedness begets vulnerability."

Or, as Joel Brenner, the former counsel to the National Security Agency explained in the *Washington Post* this past weekend: "The Internet was not built for security, yet we have made it the backbone of virtually all private-sector and government operations, as well as communications. Pervasive connectivity has brought dramatic gains in productivity and pleasure but has created equally dramatic vulnerabilities. Huge heists of personal information are common, and cybertheft of intellectual property and infrastructure penetrations continue at a frightening pace."

There was considerable agreement among the experts in this canvassing that individuals—their accounts and their identities—will be more vulnerable to cyber attacks from bad actors in the

Government Hacking

Too often, the policies and practices of law enforcement and intelligence agencies can be disastrous for security.

Attempts to weaken encryption through law, policy, or informal pressure can make technology devices less secure for everyone. Government agents may infiltrate, copy, delete, or damage data during digital investigations. The government may even actively create and disseminate malware that can damage computers. We've seen these dangerous techniques employed both in the United States and in countries around the world, and they inevitably have the same consequence: we are less secure.

Government attacks on security come in many disguises, including:

State-sponsored malware. The government will design and deploy malicious code that infects computers, a technique often employed by authoritarian governments to uncover or silence dissent.

Stockpiling or exploiting vulnerabilities. The government may find or purchase details of security vulnerabilities and then use them for investigative or "offensive" purposes. The US government has created a policy, known as the Vulnerabilities Equities Process (VEP), to decide whether to disclose information about security vulnerabilities or instead withhold this information for its own purposes. This process is opaque, leaving the public in the dark about how frequently security vulnerabilities are left unaddressed. Although the government says the process is biased in favor of disclosure, there is no requirement in the VEP to tell technology makers about their security flaws.

Promoting crypto backdoors. Whether through legislation, litigation, or unofficial pressure, government attempts to undermine crypto, defeat security features, obtain "keys" to unlock encrypted data, or insert vulnerabilities into software make us all less secure.

Malicious hacking. Whether sanctioned by a court or not, the government may actively break into computers remotely. Agents may access, copy, delete, or even create data in order to suit their needs. Too often, these practices are shrouded in secrecy with inadequate oversight by the judicial system, beginning with opaque and overbroad warrants authorizing installation of malware, all the way up to refusals to share details of the malware with defendants as part of a fair trial.

These tools can have dire consequences for the security and privacy of users who have done nothing wrong and are not even connected to an investigation. In other cases, these tools are disproportionate to the threat, wreaking havoc on users' computers when less invasive techniques would have been appropriate.

In balancing the need for strong security against the potential benefit of hacking and other anti-security techniques, the government—including the courts—must carefully consider the costs to society. The public needs to be able to access secure digital tools. And as a society, we have an interest in protecting innocent users from the collateral effects of intrusive surveillance, whether by law enforcement and intelligence agencies.

Above all, the government must be accountable to the people, and that means promoting strong crypto and security.

"Government Hacking and Subversion of Digital Security," Electronic Frontier Foundation. https://www.eff.org/issues/government-hacking-digital-security.

future and that businesses will be persistently under attack. Many said the most vulnerable targets include essential utilities. Many also believe that theft at a larger scale than is now being experienced and economic disruptions could be likely.

The experts had varying opinions about the likely extent of damage and disruption possible at the nation-state level. Many argued that cyber attacks between nations have already occurred, often citing as an example the spread of the Stuxnet worm. The respondents also invoked the Cold War as a metaphor as they anticipated the world to come. They argued that the cyber deterrence of mutually assured disruption or destruction would likely keep competing powers from being too aggressive against other nation-states. At the same time, they also anticipate the current cyber arms race dynamic will expand as nations and other groups and individuals ceaselessly work to overcome security measures through the design of potent exploits.

Some expect that opponents of the political status quo in many regions of the world will work to implement cyber attacks against governments or other entrenched institutions. One "yes" respondent, Dave Kissoondoyal, CEO for KMP Global Ltd., put it this way: "I would not say that a major cyber attack will have caused widespread harm to a nation's security and capacity to defend itself and its people, but the risks will be there. By 2025, there will be widespread use of cyber terrorism and countries will spend a lot of money on cyber security."

Some observed that the Internet's expansion will multiply vulnerabilities of all types, even inside one's home. Tim Kambitsch, an activist Internet user, wrote, "The Internet of Things is just emerging. In the future, control of physical assets, not just information, will be open to cyber attack."

Some respondents who know the technology world well, but are not privy to insider knowledge about cyber threats, expressed uncertainty about the state of things and whether the disaster scenarios that are commonly discussed are hyped or not. The vice president of research and consumer media for a research and analysis firm observed, "There are serious problems, but it's not clear that those who are directing the hype are focused on the correct problems or solutions. So, the problem is both serious and over-hyped."

Security-oriented experts expressed concerns. Jeremy Epstein, a senior computer scientist at SRI International, said, "Damages in the billions will occur to manufacturing and/or utilities but because it ramps up slowly, it will be accepted as just another cost (probably passed on to taxpayers through government rebuilding subsidies and/or environmental damage), and there will be little motivation for the private sector to defend itself. Due to political gridlock and bureaucratic inertia, the government will be unable to defend itself, even if it knows how. The issue is not primarily one of technical capability (although we're sorely lacking in that department). The primary issue is a lack of policy/political/economic incentives and willpower to address the problem."

In Russia Cyberattacks Are Used to Punish Its Former Republics

John C. K. Daly

As Russia sought to establish control over its former republics in the early 2000s, cyberattacks were launched by several sides. Russia and Ukraine traded cyberattacks, and Russian attacks on Georgia and Estonia did significant damage. Experts are unsure whether these attacks have been launched by the Russian government itself or by "patriotic hackers," individual cyber criminals who are sympathetic to their government's cause. Dr. John C. K. Daly is a Eurasian foreign affairs and defense policy expert for the Jamestown Foundation and a nonresident fellow at the Central Asia-Caucasus Institute in Washington, D.C.

As you read, consider the following questions:

1. How have conflicts between Russia and post-Soviet states spilled into cyberspace?
2. What institutions and infrastructure have been attacked within Russia and the other victimized countries?
3. How have cyberattacks changed the nature of warfare?

Rising tensions between Russia and Ukraine have spilled into cyberspace, although it remains unclear whether government

"Ukrainian-Russian Dispute Moves Into Cyberspace," by John C. K. Daly. Article first appeared in The Jamestown Foundation's publication "Eurasia Daily Monitor," Volume II, Issue 53, on March 20, 2014. Original article can be found on Jamestown.org. Reprinted by permission.

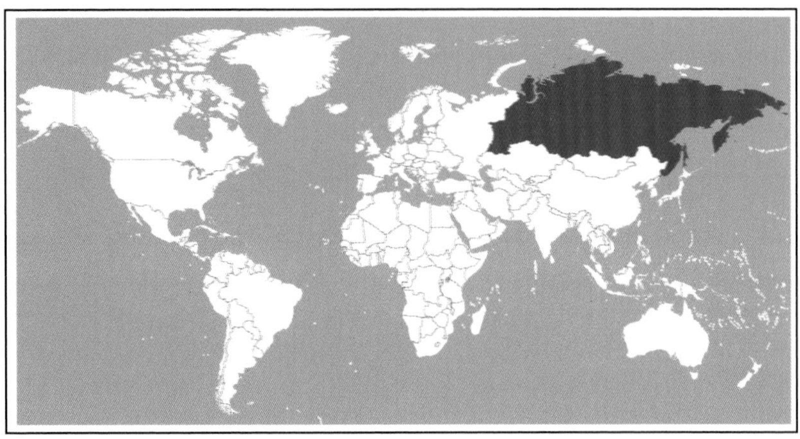

entities or lone wolf patriotic hackers are responsible. In a highly embarrassing incident, Russian President Vladimir Putin's webpage was knocked offline, even as a Kremlin source said it was unconnected with "the events in Ukraine." Other Russian websites attacked include the Bank of Russia, the Foreign Ministry and state broadcaster Channel One (http://www.dailysmi.net/news/456101/; RT, March 14). In Ukraine, cyber-assaults included the National Security and Defense Council, the Crimean Supreme Council as well as the Crimean independence referendum website (ITAR-TASS, March 11, 16). The most important casualty of the clashes so far is the free flow of information.

The current clashes echo earlier Russian political disputes with former Soviet republics. In 2007, Estonia, a member of the North Atlantic Treaty Organization (NATO), was subjected to cyber-attacks that blocked websites, froze its entire Internet infrastructure and paralyzed bank cards and mobile-phone networks. Despite Russian denials, Estonian officials were convinced of Russia's involvement. In March 2009, Duma deputy Sergei Markov stated that one of his assistants carried out the cyber-attacks (EkhoMoskvy, March 5, 2009). However, Estonian defense ministry officials dismissed Markov's assertions.

During the 2008 Georgian-Russian conflict, after Georgia shelled Tskhinvali on August 8, most South Ossetian websites went offline. Russian media, including "Russia Today" (since rebranded as just RT), were subsequently subjected to cyber-attacks. In turn, Georgian websites, including those of the president, parliament, government and the foreign ministry, were hacked. The website of then Georgian president Mikheil Saakashvili was assaulted in a wave of denial of service (DDoS) attacks from 500 IP addresses (Fond StrategicheskoiKul'tury, October 31, 2008).

According to research published by the US Cyber Consequences Unit, "The cyber-attacks against Georgian targets [in 2008] were carried out by civilians with little or no direct involvement on the part of the Russian government or military" (US Cyber Consequences Unit, "Overview by the US-CCU of the Cyber Campaign against Georgia in August of 2008," US-CCU Special Report, August 2009, pp. 2–3).

However, the situation in Ukraine today is significantly different. Much of Ukraine's telecommunications infrastructure dates from Soviet times, making it particularly vulnerable to penetration by Moscow. And even more importantly, the Russian military now has the ability to conduct offensive cyber-operations. Notably, after belatedly realizing the need for a Russian military command capable of operating in cyberspace, Putin signed legislation in 2012 establishing the Foundation for Advanced Studies—a structure, which is roughly analogous to DARPA in the United States and is designed to develop innovative technology and modernize the military-industrial complex, including in the realm of cyber-warfare capabilities (VPK, October 18, 2012; venture-news.ru, June 6, 2012).

Attacks from cyberspace on both Ukrainian and Russian targets have been escalating in earnest. On March 4, Ukrainian Security Service (SBU) head ValentynNalivaichenko said, "I can confirm that an […] attack is under way on mobile phones of members of the Ukrainian parliament for the second day in a row. At the entrance to Ukrtelecom in Crimea, illegally and in violation of all commercial contracts, equipment was installed that blocks my phone as well as the phones of other deputies, regardless of their

NATO and Russia

In addition to rediscovering some of its old skills, the [NATO] alliance faces the challenge of adapting to new threats. Foremost among them: Russia's information warfare—a strategy that current President Vladimir Putin announced after becoming prime minister in 1999. Then, Putin drew up a national security policy in which information warfare was a major plank. It was first tested in Estonia in 2007, when Russia attacked the country's vital computer networks. Since then, Estonia has been at the forefront in trying to link conventional defense with cyber and hybrid warfare in NATO.

And because Russia had tried to influence the outcome of the Dutch, the US, and the French elections, governments and independent civil society organizations are motivated to counter the barrage of fake news and propaganda spread by Russia. "Actually, there's a solid consensus among NATO countries about the insidiousness and danger of Russia's disinformation campaigns and its cyber attacks," a NATO official said. "But it's not just up to NATO to work against this. The nations must stand up for their values and defend themselves against fake news and all the ramifications of these Russia attacks," the official added. As other NATO officials argued, the alliance has neither the means nor the mandate to counter fake news. What it can do is refute, which it does, the fake stories that it knows are sent by Russian bots and that directly target NATO. For example, emails were sent to the Lithuanian government and media outlets falsely accusing German soldiers based in Lithuania of rape.

In addition to measures targeting public opinion, NATO faces increasingly more effective cyber attacks on military and civilian infrastructure. It has addressed the first challenge reasonably well by beefing up protection of its own networks. This step mirrors measures taken by individual allies. The German defense ministry, for example, created in April 2017 a new Cyber and Information Space Command that will eventually be staffed by 13,500 soldiers and civilians.

"Nato's Eastern Flank and Its Future Relationship With Russia," by Judy Dempsey, Carnegie Endowment for International Peace, October 2017.

political affiliation" (kp.ua, March 5). Whereas, on the evening of March 13, Russia's state broadcaster Channel One website was forced offline by a DDoS attack, alleging, "Our site is temporarily unavailable due to DDoS attacks from Kiev" (Gazeta.ru, March 14).

In an ominous development predating the current dispute and far more sophisticated than relatively simple DDoS attacks, since 2010 dozens of Ukrainian network servers have been attacked with the "Snake" cyber espionage malware "tool kit" (Kyiv Post, March 9). The first such attack was recorded in 2010, followed by three in 2011, six in 2012, eight in 2013 and fourteen since the beginning of 2014. Software security engineers from BAE Systems uncovered Russian characters in Snake's source code (BAE Systems Applied Intelligence, March 14).

Illustrating the very real danger of spillover in this apparent Russian-Ukrainian cyberwar, a more recently discovered Snake software variant, "Uroburos," has "Russian roots," and there are "strong indications" that the programmers behind Uroburos are the same ones that attacked US military servers in 2008 and 2011 with Agent.BTZ—an earlier version of Snake, which the Department of Defense acknowledged had infected their classified networks (antivirus.ua, March 13). Germany's G Data Software said, "Notable hints include the usage of the exact same encryption key then and now, as well as the presence of Russian language in both cases" (G Data SecurityBlog, February 28).

While so far scant evidence exists that the hacking war truly involves state players, it is expanding. On March 14, Russian Ministry of Communications experts said that they identified a location in western Ukraine as the source of an attempted cyber-attack to jam Russian TV satellite broadcasts (RIA Novosti, 15.03.2014.). Two days later, several NATO websites were hit by DDoS attacks. "CyberBerkut," named after the previous Ukrainian regime's feared riot police, claimed responsibility for hacking NATO's main website (nato.int), NATO's Cyber Defense Center (ccdcoe.org) and NATO's Parliamentary Assembly (nato-pa.int) because of the North Atlantic Alliance's "interference" in Ukraine (Utro.ru, March 16).

Earlier cyber-attacks against Estonia and Georgia showed Russia that civilian cyber campaigns cause serious economic and psychological disruptions in a target country without provoking any serious international response. In Crimea, the stakes are far higher amid rising international opposition, so it seems unlikely that Russia would want to undertake direct massive military and government-backed cyber-attacks for fear of a political backlash.

Still, on March 17, the Ukrainian acting minister of foreign affairs, Andriy Deschytsya, visited NATO for talks with Secretary General Anders Fogh Rasmussen. While the meeting was closed to the press, the cyber conflict was doubtlessly high on the agenda. But whether the cyberwar will cool down now that Ukraine is moving its military forces out of the peninsula following Russia's unilateral annexation of Crimea remains to be seen.

In North Korea Cyberterror Attacks Attract the World's Attention

Kelsey Atherton

In the following viewpoint, Kelsey Atherton argues that North Korea may be a bit player on the world stage, but nevertheless is a superpower when it comes to cyber-technology. North Korea's laser focus on protecting its leader, Kim Jong-Un, has caused its government to develop a highly sophisticated cyber presence and to launch attacks on targets such as Sony Pictures and South Korea. Kelsey Atherton is a technology writer based in Albuquerque, New Mexico. He primarily covers defense technology and unmanned vehicles. He has written articles for Fifth Domain, Defense News, Popular Science, *and* Military Times.

As you read, consider the following questions:

1. Why has North Korea excelled in cyber-technology when its economy is so minuscule?
2. What are some of North Korea's more prominent attacks?
3. How is North Korea able to pull of such attacks on major world targets?

In September 2016, North Korean intelligence services stole a huge batch of classified US and South Korean military plans—

"How North Korean hackers stole 235 gigabytes of classified US and South Korean military plans," by Kelsey Atherton, Vox.com, and Vox Media, Inc., October 13, 2017. https://www.vox.com/world/2017/10/13/16465882/north-korea-cyber-attack-capability-us-military. Reprinted by permission.

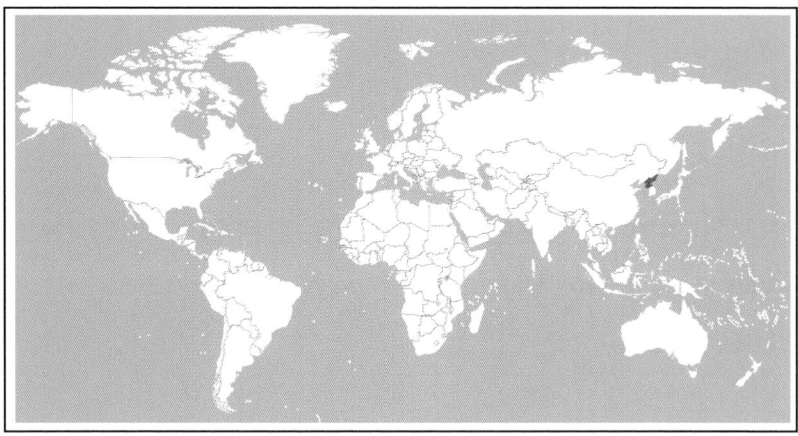

including a plan to assassinate North Korea's dictator Kim Jong Un and other top government officials.

Yet this was not the stuff of an old-school John le Carré spy novel, with shady figures in trench coats exchanging documents at a dark rendezvous spot in the woods. North Korea's data theft was done entirely through computer systems.

According to a South Korean politician, last fall North Korean hackers gained access to South Korea's Defense Integrated Data Center and stole 235 gigabytes of classified military plans. Two plans in particular stand out: One was for how to respond to an attack on South Korea by North Korean commandos. The other was the plan for what's called a "decapitation strike," or an operation that would specifically target Kim and other key government officials loyal to the regime. But the full depth of what was stolen is still unknown.

The fact that we're only just now learning of the extent of the burglary, more than a year after it happened, is a testament to North Korea's immense cyber capabilities.

But wait a second—how did an impoverished country like North Korea end up with such impressive hacking abilities? And are they really that impressive? Or is our information just really easy to steal?

It turns out that while we've been (understandably) focused on North Korea's nuclear weapons and ballistic missiles, the country has been quietly developing another powerful tool—a selection of malware and malicious code, a veritable cyberweapons cache.

How Did North Korea Pull It Off?

North Korea is one of seven nations generally regarded as "cyberpowers"—countries with the ability to mess around in the information systems of other countries. (Besides North Korea, the major cyberpowers are the United States, Russia, China, the United Kingdom, Iran, and France.)

In 2014, North Korean hackers conducted a major operation against Sony in the United States in retaliation for the Sony Pictures film *The Interview*, a Seth Rogen and James Franco comedy depicting a fictional assassination of Kim Jong Un—a cyberattack that some political commentators labeled an act of war.

This latest hack of the military documents worked through human error. As the *Wall Street Journal* reports, the North Korean hackers first gained access to a South Korean company that makes the antivirus software used by the South Korean military. That compromised antivirus software provided a path for North Korean hackers into South Korean military computers.

Normally, the military database they hacked, working on a secured intranet, would be safe from compromise—but a contractor working at the data center left a cable in place that connected the military intranet to the internet, allowing the North Korean hackers to access the database of sensitive documents.

That connection remained in place for more than a year, and wasn't detected until September 2016. North Korean state media has denied involvement in the attack, claiming instead that South Korea made up the whole thing.

How Did a Country Like North Korea Develop Such Impressive Cyber Capabilities?

Computer scientists are the key to creating and maintaining new cyberweapons, but there's also a great deal of reverse-engineering that goes on. For instance, in 2012 Iran used cyber tools to wipe

North Korea's Cyberattacks

Over the past few years, North Korea has resorted to cyber attacks to affect its adversaries with increasing scale and capacity. This trend is alarming given that advanced cyber warfare capabilities could increase North Korea's asymmetrical advantage and provide alternative means of escalating a crisis. The March 20, 2013 cyber attack on major South Korean banks and broadcasting agencies served as a wake-up call for South Korean policymakers, since North Korea not only clearly demonstrated Pyongyang's intent to utilize cyber attacks as a tool during a crisis, but also showed significant improvement in capabilities from earlier attacks that resorted to DDoS attacks on websites.

Effectively dealing with North Korea's conventional and nuclear provocations has become one of the greatest challenges for US foreign policy in the Asia-Pacific. North Korea has consistently disrupted an enduring US strategic objective to promote peace and stability in the region, not only by continuing to develop and test nuclear and missile technologies but also by initiating various conventional provocations short of war that undermines security on the Korean peninsula. For US and allies, it has been increasingly difficult to respond to such provocations in a way that demonstrates firm commitment and yet avoid unnecessary escalation, while finding mechanisms to effectively defend and deter increasingly varied means of provocations such as sinking of the Cheonan and shelling of Yeonpyeong Island.

The goal of this project is to assess North Korea's organizational and functional capability to effectively conduct offensive cyber operations, assess their strategic motivations in investing in cyber capabilities, and discuss key policy implications for US and South Korea.

"North Korea's Cyber Capabilities," Center for Strategic and International Studies.

and render useless 35,000 computers at Saudi Aramco, one of the world's biggest oil companies. The tools Iran used in the Saudi Aramco attack were largely modifications of tools that had attacked Iran, now redesigned for different targets.

"[For] everybody, once your code gets out on the internet, it's possible that someone else can intercept copy and modify for their own use," says Bob Gourley, co-founder of the security consultancy firm Cognitio and veteran of the intelligence community.

"North Koreans might be borrowing code they saw in a Russian attack," Gourley says, but that "doesn't mean Russians and North Koreans are collaborating. [It] just means they saw that code and modified it, or they may be modifying code of some hacker or some criminal groups."

"Everyone starts to build upon other people's exploits," he adds.

But North Korea has the smallest economy of all the cyberpowers, with a GDP estimated at somewhere between that of Vermont and Wyoming. How, then, can it so effectively fund the kinds of computer scientists needed to maintain such a potent cyber capability?

Part of the answer has to do with the nature of the North Korean economy itself. The North has what's known as a "command economy," which means that the central government basically controls every single aspect of the economy, including the production and distribution of goods and services.

As a result, the regime is able to direct as many resources as it wants toward military programs within the country, like its nuclear project and its cyber program, even in the face of strict foreign sanctions.

The other reason is that North Korea's cyber division actually makes a lot of money on its own, thanks to the country's willingness to have its military programmers engage in straight-up crime.

"There are remarkable similarities between North Korea and an organized crime group," says William Carter, deputy director of the technology policy program at the Center for Strategic and International Security, a Washington think tank.

For instance, Carter says, North Korea's cyber division "used a pretty sophisticated scheme to send false payment orders through the Swiss [banking] network and got hundreds of millions of dollars transferred out of the banks of Bangladesh, the Philippines, Vietnam, Ecuador, and others and into accounts controlled by North Korean government."

When your hackers are bringing in that kind of cash, paying their salaries becomes a whole lot easier.

Why Would North Korea Launch Cyberattacks?

While North Korean attacks and intrusions make headlines, it's safe to assume that all countries with the capability to do so are actively watching and tracking and spying on the cyber capabilities of other countries. So it's not the use of cyber itself that sets North Korea apart from other nations.

"The challenge is that North Korea's objectives are a lot about being able to lash out," says Michael Sulmeyer, director of the Cyber Security Project at Harvard's Belfer Center, "and they're also limited in other ways they could insert themselves, cut off from so much of the global economy."

With an army focused on the South, a navy that is limited in reach, and an air force oriented toward defense, North Korea's main ways to threaten countries beyond its immediate borders are with missiles or with cyber intrusions.

Having a robust hacking capability means that Pyongyang can attack those who make both fictional depictions of Kim Jong Un's assassination and actual military plans for such an event. Kim inherited not just his father's nuclear program but his grandfather's intense paranoia, and the whole orientation of the regime is built around ensuring his survival.

Viewpoint 4

In Ukraine a Revolution Coincided with Foreign Cyberattacks

Nikolay Koval

In the following excerpted viewpoint, cybersecurity expert Nikolay Koval discusses the cyberattacks in the Ukraine surrounding the Ukrainian revolution of 2014. Koval argues that the hackers were state-sponsored agents of the Russian government, who sought to use cyberattacks to exert control over the breakaway republic. The most serious breech was the hacking of the election, though Ukrainian countermeasures ensured that the final results were genuine. Koval argues that Ukraine must do more to guard against future attacks, which are inevitable. Nikolay Koval is a former Computer Emergency Response Team of Ukraine (CERT-UA) officer. He recently launched a cyber-security start-up.

As you read, consider the following questions:

1. According to Koval, how did the rise of cyberattacks coincide with political events?
2. How was the Ukrainian election compromised by outside interests?
3. What steps must Ukraine undertake to bolster its cybersecurity?

During Ukraine's revolution in 2014, I served our country as the chief of its Computer Emergency Response Team

"Revolution Hacking," by Nikolay Koval, NATO Cooperative Cyber Defence. Reprinted by permission.

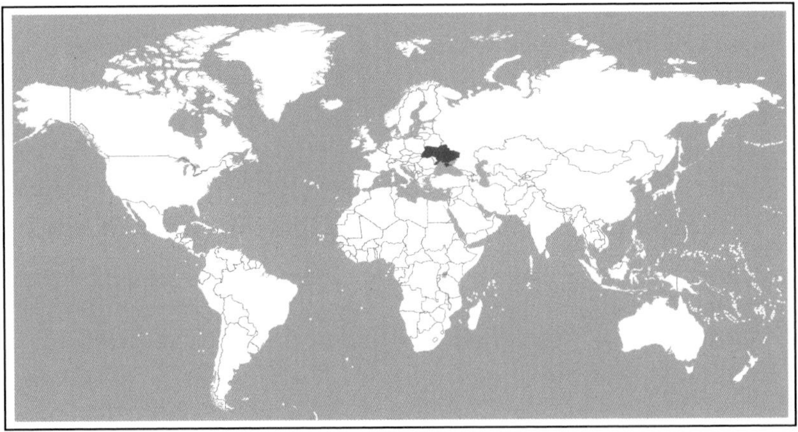

(CERT-UA).[1] During my tenure, we responded to a wide variety of network security incidents. I can say with great confidence that the number and severity of cyber attacks against Ukraine rose in parallel with ongoing political events.

Before the revolution, Ukraine experienced a fairly typical array of incidents, the most frequent of which were botnet-driven[2] Distributed Denial of Service (DDoS) attacks. Often, these came in retaliation for unpopular government initiatives, such as when the authorities tried to shut down the file-sharing website www.ex.ua. By the end of 2012, some of the public's frustration was channelled into politically motivated website "defacements" (i.e. digital graffiti) within the government's Internet Protocol (IP) space.

In 2013, we began to discover a much more serious class of malware. Network vandalism had given way to a surge in cyber espionage, for which commercial cyber security companies developed a list of colourful names: RedOctober, MiniDuke, NetTraveler, and many more.

Once the revolution began in February 2014, even ordinary Ukrainians became familiar with the combination of hacking and political activism, or "hacktivism," in which the attackers seek to wage psychological war via the internet. Although many people were exhausted by the momentous political events that had shaken our country, it was hard to ignore the publication of allegedly leaked Ukrainian government documents detailing a secret, fascist government agenda. The most prominent hacktivist group was CyberBerkut,[3] and it is their most famous attack which is detailed below.

In the course of so many incident responses we learned that, with sufficient evidence, it is usually possible to understand the general nature of an attack, including who the attackers might be and what they were seeking. Timing, context, victim identity, and malware sophistication are good indicators. Cutting-edge spyware is likely to be found on the computers of senior government officials or on important network nodes within national critical infrastructure. For example, in one case, we wondered why a private sector executive had been hit, and then discovered that he had previously been a high-ranking government official.

In my opinion, CERT-UA—in collaboration with network security firms such as Kaspersky Lab, Symantec, ESET, and others—was usually able to detect, isolate, and eliminate serious threats to network security in Ukraine.

However, in the course of our work, we also discovered another problem that any enterprise today should seek to address: a fundamental lack of user understanding of cyber security. At every institution, therefore, we tried to carry out a malware "literacy campaign" to teach employees how infections begin and how attackers can subsequently control their computers to steal documents, all via a tiny, unauthorised program that can be maddeningly difficult to find.

Case Study: Hacking a Presidential Election

The most sensational hacktivist attack took place during Ukraine's presidential elections. On 21 May 2014, CyberBerkut compromised the Central Election Commission (CEC), disabling core CEC network nodes and numerous components of the election system. For nearly 20 hours, the so ware, which was designed to display real-time updates in the vote count, did not work properly.

On 25 May—election day—12 minutes before the polls closed (19:48 EET), the attackers posted on the CEC website a picture of Ukrainian Right Sector leader Dmitry Yarosh, incorrectly claiming that he had won the election. His image was immediately shown on Russian TV channels.

It is important to note here that this attack could in no way have determined the outcome of the election. In Ukraine, every citizen inks his or her vote on a real paper ballot, and all votes are manually verified. Each polling station in every corner of the country physically delivers its ballots to CEC headquarters in Kyiv for aggregation, reconciliation, and determination of the final tally. CEC's information technology (IT) infrastructure is a complex, geographically distributed system designed for fault tolerance and transparency. Polling stations have an "anti-fraud" design that allows monitors to detect anomalies such as dramatically swinging vote counts and report them to the appropriate authorities. Any serious disruption during an election would generate immediate suspicion about its legitimacy, and spark a desire for a new election.

That said, I believe that we should not underestimate the ability of hackers—especially those that enjoy state sponsorship—to disrupt the political process of a nation. If CEC's network had not been restored by 25 May, the country would simply have been unable to follow the vote count in real-time. However, to what extent would that have caused citizens to question the integrity of the entire process? It is hard to know.

CEC was not the only election-related site compromised. There were many others, including some that were only tangentially related to Ukrainian politics when, for example, the word "election" had unfortunately appeared somewhere on the site. But even when attacks against low-level sites were unsophisticated, and the sites basically continued to function, the attackers still got the press attention they sought.

The technical aspects of this hack also tell us something very important: the hackers were professionals. Beyond disabling the site and successfully displaying incorrect election results, CERT-

UA discovered advanced cyber espionage malware on the CEC network (Sofacy/APT28/Sednit). These two aspects of the attack—disruption and espionage—may seem contradictory, but in fact they are quite complementary. Hackers must first conduct in-depth reconnaissance of a target prior to any serious attack.

To bolster its technical credentials as an elite hacker group, CyberBerkut claimed to have discovered and exploited a "zero-day" vulnerability in CEC's Cisco ASA software. In my opinion, it is highly unlikely that a non-state hacker group would possess such a high level of technical expertise. If CyberBerkut really did exploit a zero-day, the group is likely supported by a nation-state.

During my tenure as chief of CERT-UA, the CEC compromise was probably the most technically advanced cyber attack we investigated. It was well planned, highly targeted, and had some (albeit limited) real-world impact. Preparation for such an attack does not happen overnight; based on our analysis of Internet Protocol (IP) activity, the attackers began their reconnaissance in mid-March 2014—more than two months prior to the election. Neither does the level of required expertise suggest that this was the work of amateurs; at a minimum, the hackers had gained administrator-level access to CEC's network.

Conclusion: What Is to Be Done?

Ukraine today faces cyber security challenges on at least two fronts. First, there are technical attacks against a wide range of network infrastructure, including individual websites and whole Internet Service Providers (ISPs). These encompass everything from preoperational reconnaissance to social engineering against the target's employees. Second, there is an ongoing, content-driven information war within the online media space designed to influence and deceive the public.

More serious threats lie over the horizon. In recent incident response activities we have discovered samples of the most advanced forms of malware, including BlackEnergy2/SandWorm, Potao, Turla/Urobros, and more.

In the face of these threats, Ukraine is currently unprepared. At the strategic level, our senior officials are preoccupied with more pressing concerns. At the tactical level, our law enforcement agencies still fail to grasp the basic connection between email attachments, remote administrative so ware, and cyber espionage. Today, there is no unified mechanism to monitor Ukraine's network space, which hinders our ability to detect cases of unauthorised access in a timely fashion.

It is time for the government of Ukraine to pay greater attention to cyber security. Given our current national security crisis, this will not be easy. However, in spite of the challenging environment, many positive developments are taking place in Ukraine, such as the recent transformation of Kyiv's metropolitan police force.[4] A similar breakthrough can take place in our cyber security domain, but it must begin with the allocation of funds to hire and retain the right personnel through competitive salaries and more attractive working conditions.

Endnotes

1. CERT-UA lies within the State Service for Special Communications and Information Protection of Ukraine.
2. In other words, the botnets were large enough that no other amplification was needed.
3. For background on this hacker group, see Wikipedia entry "CyberBerkut," https://en.wikipedia.org/wiki/CyberBerkut.
4. Laura Mills. "In Ukraine's Capital, a New Show of Force," *Wall Street Journal*, August 6, 2015, http://www.wsj.com/articles/ in-ukraines-capital-a-new-show-of-force-1438903782.

Viewpoint 5

In Ukraine Reports of Cyberwar Are Overblown

Martin Libicki

In the following excerpted viewpoint, Martin Libicki argues that while the expectations for cyberwarfare are strong any time an international conflict breaks out, such as that in Ukraine, there has been a marked absence of major cyberattacks. Libicki believes that the hype conserning cyberterrorism is currently overstated. Nevertheless, the internet being in its infancy, the current state of internet affairs is not predictive of the future. Martin C. Libicki is professor at the Frederick S. Pardee RAND Graduate School in Santa Monica, California. He is also a distinguished visiting professor at the US Naval Academy and has published widely in the field of cybersecurity.

As you read, consider the following questions:

1. Why is the expectation of cyberwar so strong when political upheavals occur?
2. What are the reasons why no major cyberattack has occurred in the Ukranian conflict?
3. According to Libicki, why is the current lack of a major cyberattack not predictive of the future?

For the last twenty years, with the advent of serious thinking about "cyber war," most analysts—and even the more sceptical

"The Cyber War that Wasn't," by Martin Libicki, NATO Cooperative Cyber Defence. Reprinted by permission.

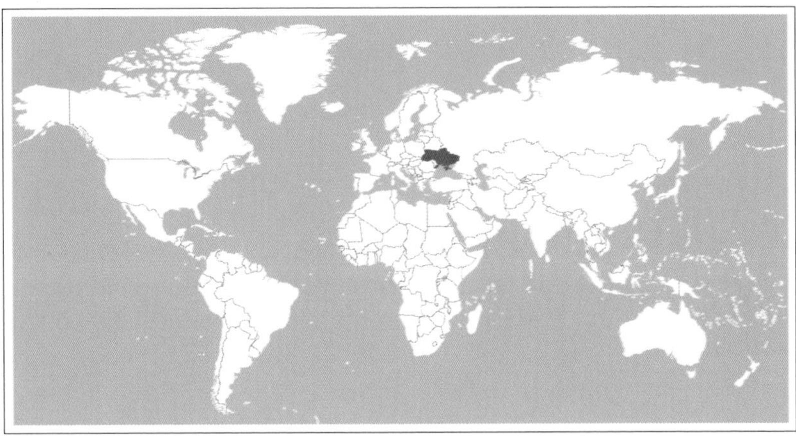

thinkers—have been convinced that all future kinetic wars between modern countries would have a clear cyber component. However, the current Russo-Ukrainian conflict is challenging this widely held notion.

Coinciding with this assumption, however, it must be said that within the past generation there have been few conflicts in which both sides appeared both capable of and vulnerable to cyber attack. Either one party to the conflict—usually the United States—held all the cyber cards, or neither did. For cyber war to take place, at least one side must have enough digitised networked equipment to make much difference. In some past conflicts, the US may have abstained from firing digital weapons because the other side simply lacked appropriate targets.

Many analysts have speculated that the US, and now other highly networked societies, may hesitate to use cyber tactics because of their own inherent vulnerabilities in this domain.

Apart from Stuxnet, the most frequently cited example of cyber war in action came during an alleged Israel Air Force strike against Syrian nuclear facilities in 2007. Integrated air-defence systems (IADS) have been considered ripe targets for cyber warfare, but it was understood that there would be a cost-benefit analysis relative to dispatching them using more familiar tools such as electronic warfare or missiles. There were rumours, for example, that the US employed cyberwar techniques against Serbian IADS in 1999, but these rumours were never substantiated. Even the Syrian story may be a fairy tale, as the details are classified and subject to much speculation. It is possible that the tactics were in fact more conventional, such as traditional jamming.[1]

Unique Aspects of the Russo-Ukrainian Conflict

The current Russo-Ukrainian conflict, however, is a different case, and it should help us to understand if cyber war is, in 2015, more myth or reality. According to the prevailing assumption, this war should have seen serious and open cyber war strategies and tactics. Both countries have technologically advanced societies and weaponry that at least came up to 1990 standards of modernity. Both countries have a strong information technology (IT) base, and hackers a-plenty, although many of them are engaged in organised crime rather than working for the state.[2] Russia's state-sponsored hackers are widely believed to be on par with, or very close to, NSA-level standards.

The most notable thing about the war in Ukraine, however, is the near-complete absence of any perceptible cyber war. There has been vigorous cyber espionage,[3] the targeting of cell phones by Russian electronic warfare, and the use of old-fashioned bolt-cutters to sever lines of communication in Crimea.[4] Patriotic hacktivists on both sides have conducted harassing but small cyber attacks against each other,[5] both sides have conducted Distributed Denial-of-Service (DDoS) attacks (e.g., by Russia against Ukraine's parliament),[6] and a (fruitless) campaign to corrupt voting processes in Ukraine.[7] However, we have seen nothing comparable to the cyber attacks carried out against Estonia in 2007 or Georgia in 2008.

On the other hand, the information and propaganda war in the social media domain (particularly from the Russian side) has been relentless. In this regard, Moscow has a competitive advantage over Kyiv. The two countries share a common language, Russian (the use of the Ukrainian language is growing fast, but that language is Slavic), and most Russian-language-friendly sites such as *VKontakte* (the Russian Facebook) are headquartered in Russia. That said, little if any of the conflict taking place in social media requires subverting computers through the discovery of vulnerabilities or the engagement of exploits.

In particular, there are two major forms of cyber attack that have not taken place in the Russo-Ukrainian conflict: attacks on critical infrastructure and attacks on defence systems. It is possible that, in the future, we may learn that there have been such attacks, but that they were simply subtle enough to slip under the radar. With Stuxnet, Iran's centrifuge plant at Natanz was infected for six months, with centrifuges failing at unexpected rates, before Iranian engineers understood why. Successful cyber attacks could indefinitely be ascribed to incompetent management before a complete picture is understood. And as for military systems, credible stories of their successful attacks may emerge years later, when people are freer to talk about what happened in the war.

Even with all of that in mind, in the Internet era it has become difficult to keep secrets for long periods of time, and the growing absence of cyber attack evidence is turning into the evidence of absence.

Possible Reasons for the Absence of Cyber Conflict

So, based on what we know now, why has this kinetic conflict seen so little cyber conflict? Here are some possible answers to that question.

Ukraine does not have the requisite hackers

Russian hackers need no introduction. They work for the state, for cyber crime syndicates, and for themselves as patriotic hacktivist defenders of Mother Russia. However, on the Ukrainian side (a much smaller nation to begin with), it is possible that a large percentage of the hacker talent is of Russian descent and may have divided loyalties in this conflict. That said, many small countries have made large contributions in cyberspace, including Estonia, Iceland, Lebanon[8] and Israel.

Neither Russia nor Ukraine has valid targets

This gets closer to the truth. Although the Soviet Union of 1990 had sophisticated weapons, their long suits were in metallurgy and radio-frequency devices. When the Soviet Union collapsed, it was significantly behind the West in terms of electronics and so ware. In the last five years, there has been a modest recapitalisation in Russia, but close to none in Ukraine. Since the end of the Cold War, the United States has for the most part maintained its substantial lead over Russia in digitisation and networking. Thus, US fears about its systems falling prey to hackers are currently not shared by the majority of nation-states, who feel that they are not particularly vulnerable. However, the truth probably lies somewhere in the middle: for example, no one is buying analogue telecommunications systems anymore, not even in the developing world. New equipment is digital and networked, not only because it is more powerful, but because it is cheaper over the long run. Therefore, even in Russia and Ukraine, the level of digitisation is likely high enough to engender real concerns about their societies' vulnerability to cyber attack. Their militaries may be antiquated, but due to the close relationship between the IT of modern civilian and military domains, there is probably still plenty for hackers to target.

There is no need—the Russians already own Ukraine

Much of Ukraine's infrastructure—notably the phone system—dates from the Soviet era. It is logical, therefore, that the Russians have already wired the phone system for interception and, it would hardly be in their interest to take it down.[9] This explanation does not explain anything the Ukrainian side has or has not done, nor does it explain the lack of attacks on other systems such as power, natural gas distribution or finance. However, it may help to understand a lack of attacks on telecommunications, given that a cyber attack could disrupt a lucrative cyber espionage operation by alerting defenders that their systems have been penetrated and forcing a system scrub. Such action may not only knock out existing implants but also make the reinsertion of malware more difficult. effects of cyber attack tend to be short term, while stealthy cyber exploitation can persist for years. Therefore, for strategic purposes, attacks such as Denial-of-Service (DoS) can be counterproductive. Well-designed technologies like Skype, however, which have end-to-end encryption, could lessen the value of cyber espionage over time (but not by much, because encryption does not protect if computers on one or both ends of the conversation are compromised), and increase the likelihood of denial-of-service attacks.

Neither Russia nor Ukraine wants such an escalation

In theory, the Russo-Ukrainian conflict is not a war between two states, but an insurgency and counter-insurgency campaign over territory in eastern Ukraine. According to the Russian Government, Russian forces are not even in the fight, and thus far, neither country's infrastructure (outside the battle zone) has been touched. In this context, if Russia were to attack Ukraine's infrastructure or vice versa it would be hard to ascribe the attack to separatists, who likely would not possess the requisite advanced hacker skills among their "patriotic hacker" ranks. Organised crime syndicates may have the technical expertise, but may lack the trust or the intelligence-informed approach required. Still, given that both of these groups enjoy some state protection in Russia, such an operation is not out of the question. The more important point here is that any such escalation could change the narrative of the conflict from an inter-ethnic squabble to an interstate war. An obvious attack by Russia against Ukraine's infrastructure may conflict with its current political narrative. A Ukrainian attack against Russia could be a warning signal to Moscow that it will have to pay a price for its actions (a sporty move indeed), as well as a sign that it cannot do better in a conventional fight with the Russian military. A wild card here is that cyber war techniques in 2015 may be viewed in and of themselves as unduly escalatory, but this fear likely does not apply to cyber attacks precisely focused on enemy military targets in theatre where their use ought to seem no more alarming than the use of, say, electronic warfare. Finally, it is important to remember that two nuclear states may easily prefer fighting without resorting to nuclear weapons; in cyber warfare, many analysts have noted that any two sides are likely riddled with exploitable vulnerabilities.[10]

Cyber war is not a "silver bullet"

Proponents of cyber war argue that attacks are cheap, asymmetric, effective, and risk-free. But what if they are wrong? A truly successful cyber attack—one that does more than simply annoy defenders—is harder than it looks. Penetrating systems without getting caught requires technical expertise that is in short supply. Preoperational reconnaissance and intelligence gathering of the kind required to create politically interesting effects such as against national critical infrastructure, or to target military defence systems takes a long time and may not produce practical results. In 2015, it is also possible that neither Russian nor Ukrainian systems are sufficiently wired to allow for easy access and manipulation. Human-in-the-loop safeguards, for example, may prevent truly serious damage from occurring except on rare occasions. Both critical infrastructure and combat systems are designed to operate under a great deal of stress and unexpected events. Some states may already have calculated that the effects of cyber war are limited, temporary, and hard to repeat. Attackers also fear that digital weapons may work only once before defenders can plug the necessary holes. In this light, is developing a cyber war arsenal really worth it?

Conclusion

In 1972, when Chinese Premier Zhou Enlai was asked about the significance of the French Revolution of 1789, he famously said, 'It is too soon to say."[11] With that logic in mind, it must be noted that the Internet is still a baby, and that cyber attacks are still in a nascent stage. Despite the prevailing 25 May 2015 ceasefire, the Russo-Ukrainian conflict is not over. Currently, it could be that neither side wants to escalate this somewhat localised conflict into the realm of interstate war, and this may inhibit operations otherwise warranted in less opaque circumstances. Both parties to the conflict are still exploring their best options, and both are surely upgrading their traditional and digital military arsenals. Finally, it is hard to say what current cyber operations may come to light in the future. However, in mid-2015, the preponderance of evidence suggests that the easy assumption that cyber attacks would unquestionably be used in modern warfare has come up wanting.

Endnotes

1. As Richard Clarke and Robert Knake maintain in *Cyberwar, The Next Threat to National Security and What to Do About It*, New York, NY: HarperCollins, 2010; see also David Makovsky. "The Silent Strike: How Israel bombed a Syrian nuclear installation and kept it secret," *The New Yorker*, 17 September 2012, http://www.newyorker.com/magazine/2012/09/17/the-silent-strike.
2. Ukraine's hackers do not make as much news but consider Dan Goodin. "Strange snafu hijacks UK nuke maker's traffic, routes it through Ukraine," *ARS Technica UK*, 13 March 2015, http://arstechnica.com/security/2015/03/mysterious-snafu-hijacks-uk-nukes-makers-traffic-through-ukraine/.
3. Apparently, the Russians have developed some powerful malware for that purpose against Ukraine: cyber-snake (aka Ouroboros). See Sam Jones. "Cyber Snake plagues Ukraine networks," *FT Online*, 7 March 2014, in http://www.ft.com/cms/s/0/615c-29ba-a614-11e3-8a2a-00144feab7de.html or David Sanger and Steven Erlanger, "Suspicion Falls on Russia as 'Snake' Cyber-attacks Target Ukraine's Government" *NY Times Online*, 8 March 2014, http://www.nytimes.com/2014/03/09/world/europe/ suspicion-falls-on-russia-as-snake-cyberattacks-target-ukraines-government.html.
4. Sam Jones. "Kremlin alleged to wage cyber warfare on Kiev," *FT Online*, 5 June 2014, http://www.ft.com/intl/cms/s/0/e504e278-e29d-11e3-a829-00144feabdc0.html#axzz3b4c6egXI. See also the claim of General Breedlove, EUCOM's Commander: "They disconnected the Ukrainian forces in Crimea from their command and control," from Michael Gordon. "NATO Commander Says He Sees Potent Threat From Russia," *NY Times Online*, 2 April 2014, http://www.nytimes.com/2014/04/03/world/europe/nato-general-says-russian-force-poised-to-invade-ukraine.html.
5. "'Cyber Berkut' Hackers Target Major Ukrainian Bank," *The Moscow Times*, 4 June 2014, http://www.themoscowtimes.com/business/article/cyber-berkut-hackers-target-major-ukrainian-bank/502992.html of July 4, 2014.
6. Nicole Perloth. "Cyberattacks Rise as Ukraine Crisis Spills to Internet," *New York Times Bits*, 4 March 2014, http://bits.blogs.nytimes.com/2014/03/04/cyberattacks-rise-as-ukraine-crisis-spills-on-the-internet/.
7. Mark Clayton. "Ukraine election narrowly avoided 'wanton destruction' from hackers," *Christian Science Monitor*, 17 June 2014, http://www.csmonitor.com/World/Passcode/2014/0617/Ukraine-election-narrowly-avoided-wanton-destruction-from-hackers-video.

8. Kelly Jackson Higgins. “Lebanon Believed behind Newly Uncovered Cyber Espionage Operation,” *Information Week*, 31 March 2015, http://www.darkreading.com/attacks-breaches/lebanon-believed-behind-newly-uncovered-cyber-espionage-operation/d/d-id/1319695.
9. Jeffrey Carr, quoted in Patrick Tucker. “Why Ukraine Has Already Lost The Cyberwar, Too,” *Defence One*, 28 April 2014, http:// www.defenseone.com/technology/2014/04/why-ukraine-has-already-lost-cyberwar-too/83350/.
10. “The Russians and Ukrainians have some of the best computer people in the world, because of the Soviet legacy military industrial complex,” says Taras Kuzio, a Ukraine expert at the School of Advanced International Studies at Johns Hopkins University. “These [Ukrainian] guys are fantastic. So if the Russians tried something like a cyberattack, they would get it right back. There would be some patriotic hackers in Ukraine saying, ‘Just who are the Russians to do this to us?’ from Mark Clayton. ‘Where are the cyberattacks? Russia’s curious forbearance in Ukraine,” *Christian Science Monitor*, 3 March 2014, http://www.csmonitor.com/World/Security-Watch/2014/0303/Where-are-the-cyberattacks-Russia-s-curious-forbearance-in-Ukraine.-video.
11. Alas, one of the greatest quotes in international relations of the 20th century may have been misunderstood, as Chou was actually referring to French protests of 1968. However, a diplomat present at the time said Chou’s comment was “too delicious to invite correction.” Dean Nicholas “Zhou Enlai’s Famous Saying Debunked,” *History Today*, 15 June 2011, http://www.history-today.com/blog/news-blog/dean-nicholas/zhou-enlais-famous-saying-debunked.

Periodical and Internet Sources Bibliography

The following articles have been selected to supplement the diverse views presented in this chapter.

Hyeong-wook Boo, "An Assessment of North Korean Cyber Threats." *Journal of East Asian Affairs*, Spring/Summer 2017, Vol. 31, Issue 1, pp. 97–117. www.nids.mod.go.jp/english/event/symposium/pdf/2016/E-02.pdf.

David Frost, "Espionage expert offers five viewpoints on state-sponsored hacking." *CSO*, April 4, 2017. https://www.cso.com.au/article/617077/espionage-expert-offers-five-viewpoints-state-sponsored-hacking/.

Andy Greenberg, "North Korea's Sloppy, Chaotic Cyberattacks Also Make Perfect Sense." *Wired*, June 15, 2017. https://www.wired.com/story/north-korea-cyberattacks/.

David Kushner, "The Real Story of Stuxnet." *Spectrum,* February 26, 2013. https://spectrum.ieee.org/telecom/security/the-real-story-of-stuxnet.

Owen Matthews, "Russia's Greatest Weapon May Be Its Hackers." *Newsweek,* May 7, 2015. http://www.newsweek.com/2015/05/15/russias-greatest-weapon-may-be-its-hackers-328864.html.

Khatuna Mshvidobadze, "State-sponsored Cyber Terrorism: Georgia's Experience." Georgian Security Analysis Center. September 29, 2011.

Stuart MacDonald, Lee Jarvis, and Lella Nouri, "State Cyberterrorism: A Contradiction in Terms?" *Journal of Terrorism Research* 6(3), 2015: pp. 62–75. http://doi.org/10.15664/jtr.1162.

Ankit Panda, "North Korea's Internet Outage: Whodunit?" *Diplomat*, December 23, 2014. https://thediplomat.com/2014/12/north-koreas-internet-outage-whodunit/.

Catherine A. Theohary and John W. Rollins, "Cyberwarfare and Cyberterrorism: In Brief." Congressional Research Service, March 27, 2015. https://fas.org/sgp/crs/natsec/R43955.pdf.

Kim Zetter, "An Unprecedented Look at Stuxnet, the World's First Digital Weapon." *Wired*, November 3, 2014. https://www.wired.com/2014/11/countdown-to-zero-day-stuxnet/.

Chapter 3

Profiteering from Ransomware

VIEWPOINT 1

WannaCry Ransomware Wreaked Havoc on Computers Worldwide

James Doubek

In the following viewpoint, James Doubek examines the infamous WannaCry ransomware attacks of 2017. The ransomware held users' computers hostage until they paid a substantial sum to regain their data. While the hackers did not reap a substantial monetary reward from their crime, effects of the hack were felt worldwide, and their work has led governments and organizations to reconsider their monetary commitment to internet security. Several months after this report, the United States, Canada, New Zealand, and Japan blamed North Korea for the attacks, but that country denies responsibility. James Doubek works for National Public Radio. He started at NPR as a part-time production assistant in 2015 before joining full time as an associate producer in 2017.

As you read, consider the following questions:

1. How does ransomware, or malware work?
2. Why was the WannaCry malware significant?
3. What do experts counsel with regard to whether victims should pay the ransom? Why?

The ransomware attack unleashed on Friday has affected more than 100,000 organizations in 150 countries, according to Europe's law enforcement agency Europol on Sunday.

The malware, which locks files and asks for payment to unlock them, hit businesses and institutions across the world, including shipper FedEx, train systems in Germany, a Spanish telecommunications company, universities in Asia, Russia's interior ministry and forced hospitals in Britain to turn away patients.

More than 200,000 people around the world have been affected by the malware, Jake Cigainero reports for NPR's Newscast. "The recent attack is at an unprecedented level and will require a complex international investigation to identify the culprits," Europol said in a statement. As employees return to work on Monday and turn on their computers, the number of infections could rise, the agency said.

The malware, which has been called multiple names including WannaCry, WannaDecryptor or WannaCrypt, creates a pop-up window informing users that their files are encrypted and are no longer accessible—without a payment. Screenshots of the malware show an initial request for $300 to be paid in bitcoin, with a timer that says the ransom amount will rise if it's not paid within a certain time frame, and files will be lost after that.

The hacker's total take from the global outbreak, however, appears to be much smaller than anticipated. Security researcher Brian Krebs wrote that as of Saturday, evidence showed about $26,000 in payments to the bitcoin accounts associated with the malware. "One of the nice things about Bitcoin is that anyone can view all of the historic transactions tied a given Bitcoin payment address. As a result, it's possible to tell how much the criminals at the helm of this crimeware spree have made so far and how many victims have paid the ransom," Krebs writes.

> A review of the three payment addresses hardcoded into the Wanna ransomware strain indicates that these accounts to date have received 100 payments totaling slightly more than 15 Bitcoins—or approximately $26,148 at the current Bitcoin-to-dollars exchange rate.

A "Sinkhole" that Saves

A young security researcher in the U.K., identified only as MalwareTech has claimed credit for stemming the initial outbreak.

The researcher wrote a blog post detailing the creation of a new domain as a "sinkhole" for the ransomware. The malware attempts "to connect to the domain we registered and if the connection is not successful it ransoms the system, if it is successful the malware exits," MalwareTech wrote.

The researcher added:

> [B]ecauseWannaCrypt used a single hardcoded domain, my registartion [sic] of it caused all infections globally to believe they were inside a sandbox and exit...thus we initially unintentionally prevented the spread and and further ransoming of computers infected with this malware. Of course now that we are aware of this, we will continue to host the domain to prevent any further infections from this sample.
>
> One thing that is very important to note is our sinkholing only stops this sample and there is nothing stopping them removing the domain check and trying again, so it's incredibly importiant [sic] that any unpatched systems are patched as quickly as possible.

The ransomware exploited a security flaw in Microsoft's Windows operating system. Microsoft released a patch back in March, but many users and organizations had not updated their systems with the the fix.

That prediction seemed to be borne out Sunday. Cybersecurity researcher Darien Huss, whom MalwareTech credited with assisting in stopping the first outbreak, tweeted Sunday morning that a new outbreak could be oncoming, as likely copycats released an updated version of the ransomware, without the previously used "kill switch."

Worldwide Lockout

Any halting of the initial spread, however, does not help with computers already infected.

Protect Yourself from Ransomware Attacks

"Ransomware attacks are not only proliferating, they're becoming more sophisticated," the FBI notes in a new warning. "Because email systems got better at filtering out spam, cyber criminals turned to spear phishing emails targeting specific individuals," sending more believable correspondence that addresses you by name.

...follow these best practices for everyday computer users:

1. Regularly back up the contents of your computer with an external hard drive or CD-ROM. If you keep offline copies of important files, photographs and the like, ransomware scams will have limited impact.
2. Use reputable antivirus software and a firewall. Keep software updated and set to accept security patches, as they become available, to combat ransomware and other threats. Run scans several times a week, if not daily.
3. Click wisely. Don't click on any emails or attachments you don't recognize, and carefully read body text and links, looking for spelling and grammatical errors. Some malware-laden links purport to come from legitimate businesses, but the sender's address may end in Gmail.com, Hotmail.com or another free email service.
4. Enable pop-up blockers. Criminals regularly use pop-ups to spread malicious software. Preventing pop-ups is easier than making accidental clicks on or within them.
5. Avoid free online offers for screen savers and games unless you download them from trusted websites.
6. Go to the real source. If you are expecting a delivery (or news that one was made on your behalf), don't trust "proof" provided in emailed links. Go to Amazon.com, FedEx.com, UPS.com, USPS.com, etc., for legitimate tracking or delivery news.

"New Threats in Ransomware," by Sid Kirchheimer, AARP, May 6, 2016.

Students at universities in China were locked out of their work, including dissertations and thesis papers, according to Chinese media and reported by The Associated Press.

In Germany, train operator Deutsche Bahn wrote on Twitter that signboards in stations were affected, though no train operations were affected. French automaker Renault had to temporarily shut down manufacturing at plants in northern France and Romania, Reuters reported. Among others affected, according to Reuters, include:

- Hundreds of computers at a hospital in Jakarta, Indonesia
- telecommunications companies in Spain, Portugal and Argentina
- signs at malls in Singapore
- hundreds of hospitals in the U.K.'s National Health Service

U.K. politicians are harnessing the attacks to criticize the U.K.'s Conservative Party of Prime Minister Theresa May, which made cuts to the NHS system, Willem Marx reports for NPR's Newscast unit. The cuts made NHS computer systems "outdated and vulnerable" to attack, critics say.

"Defence Minister Michael Fallon told the BBC that British authorities are spending more than $60 million on safeguarding computer systems," at the NHS, Marx adds. "Mr. Fallon said the government had already identified cyberattacks as one of the three greatest threats to Britain's security, and had pledged almost 2 and a half billion dollars to protect IT infrastructure."

Ransomware Is Big Business

Ransomware works by hijacking a person's files and threatening to delete them without payment. The latest outbreak seems to be the biggest by far, though security experts have been warning about the risks of ransomware, especially to businesses, for some time.

A report by IBM in December found 40 percent of spam emails contained ransomware attachments last year, up from less than 1 percent the previous year. The technology has been "increasingly rampant since 2014," the study says, though the concept goes back to 1989, "when PC-locking malcode was snail-mailed to victims on floppy disks." The average ransom request is $500, IBM found.

The FBI said victims incurred costs of $209 million in the first three months of 2016, Reuters reported. The US government says more than 4,000 ransomware attacks happen every day.

The government recommends reporting ransomware immediately to the FBI or the US Secret Service, and advises against paying ransoms, saying that payment is no guarantee of recovering data, and that it only encourages further attacks.

The IBM study found, however, that seven in 10 victims end up paying to get their data back. The FBI says the typical ransom runs between $200 and $10,000. Of the victims surveyed by IBM, more than half paid more than $10,000 in ransom.

The government recommends strong prevention measures as the best defense against ransomware attacks, including: strong spam filters, making sure software is patched and up to date, using anti-virus software, and regularly backing up data.

WannaCry Failed to Turn Much of a Profit

Bill Buchanan

In the following viewpoint Bill Buchanan argues that, despite the uproar and panic surrounding WannaCry, the cyberattack actually didn't generate much of a ransom. One reason it failed to collect more in ransom money is that it hit large corporations and organizations that regularly back up their data, making it nearly impossible to hold their data hostage in exchange for money. Still, the author notes, ransomware is a simple and relatively foolproof operation, making it a nearly "perfect crime." When it hits individuals and smaller organizations that lack the resources to regularly back up their data, it can be devastating—or at least bad enough to extract a healthy ransom with little chance of being caught if done correctly. Bill Buchanan is head of The Cyber Academy and professor in the School of Computing at Edinburgh Napier University.

As you read, consider the following questions:

1. Why wasn't WannaCry malware very sophisticated, according to the author?
2. What had the ransom totaled at the time the viewpoint was written?
3. What does the author consider the most frightening statistic about ransomware?

The WannaCry cyber-attack led to panic across the globe, showing just how important it is for organisations to have secure operating systems. This was not even the most sophisticated malware around. Numerous networks could easily cope with it and it largely hit legacy operating systems such as Windows XP.

In most corporate infrastructures, there would be no sign of Windows XP—and it seems unbelievable from a security perspective that the national health service of an advanced economy such as the UK would run its critical infrastructure on such an unsafe, antiquated system.

But perhaps the most striking aspect of this recent attack is how unsuccessful it has been in terms of generating a ransom. As well as the NHS in the UK, it hit French car manufacturer Renault, US delivery service FedEx, Russia's interior ministry and Spanish telecoms and gas companies. Yet ransom payments currently appear to total less than US$100,000.

This is minuscule when we compare it to other ransomware attacks. CryptoWall made its author US$325m with over 406,000 attempted infections.

The interesting thing about the WannaCry ransomware is that it mostly hit large organisations with legacy networks—and they will often not pay ransoms as they have backups or run their data from a central server. Thus, despite more than 200,000 infections worldwide, there have been fewer than 200 payments.

The weak impact is because this is a different type of ransomware. The most successful ones spread through spear phishing emails and target individuals and small businesses, which often do not have back-ups. This ransomware was different in that it spread of its own accord through unpatched systems (systems that had not followed recent warnings to protect against a virus and back-up their files)—as a worm. But it is humans that are generally the weakest link when it comes to information security.

The Perfect Crime?

Ransomware is almost the perfect IT crime. If an online criminal can trick you into installing malware, they can then lock your files and hold them ransom until you pay them a release fee. Only a secret encryption key, which they hold, can release the files.

It is simple, but highly effective. No virus scanner or law enforcement professional will be able to unlock your files unless they have the magic encryption key, and the longer the target takes to pay for it, the greater the risk there is to their business. As with any malware, though, there might be bugs in the software, so there's no guarantee that you'll get your files back, even if you do as the blackmailers say. And there's always the risk that they will just ask for more money once you pay them. Some malware increases its ransom demands over time, ultimately deleting all the files affected.

Nonetheless, it means that the success rate of the crime is incredibly high—at around 65%, as sensitive and important documents are often the target of the infection.

Increasing Infections

Computer security firm Trend Micro surveyed over 300 IT decision makers in the UK in September 2016 and found that 44% of businesses have been affected by ransomware over the last two years. The same survey found 79 new types of ransomware in the first nine months of that year. This compared to just 29 in the whole of 2015.

This is a great worry for many companies. The impact on those affected by the infection can be costly, with an average of 33 person hours taken to fix it.

In around 20% of the cases, £1,000 was requested, with an overall average of £540. Some large organisations faced demands of as much as £1m. But for many companies, this is the tip of the iceberg as it can be costly for a company in terms of reputation as customers could start seeing them as untrustworthy.

Perhaps the most frightening statistic that Trend Micro found was that in one in five cases, even when the company paid the ransom, they were unable to recover their important files—indicating that the ransomware service is not quite as robust as it should be.

If you ask many security professionals, the recent WannaCry ransomware was fairly easy to defend against, and was fairly unsophisticated. What it clearly shows is that there is still more success in tricking individuals than in spreading malware across large networks. The NHS does, though, need to make sure that not one unpatched computer ever goes near its network, and that employees understand that they shouldn't click on suspicious links.

Meanwhile, with law enforcement agencies focused on the three Bitcoin wallets associated with WannaCry to try and find out who profits, there will be a whole lot more ransomware that goes unreported and unnoticed.

In the United States a Ransomware Victim Relates His Story

Chris Rusby

In the following viewpoint, attorney Chris Rusby provides a personal account of a ransomware attack on his computer. The attack came suddenly and unexpectedly, and it infected a computer that he used for home and work. Included among the files were numerous irreplaceable family photos. Rusby was at first inclined to pay the ransom, but when sites began asking for passwords for bank accounts and similar sensitive material, he balked. The author ultimately decided not to pay, sacrificing the family photographs and other personally valuable files. Chris Rusby is a litigation and business law attorney with Rusby Law in Reno, Nevada.

As you read, consider the following questions:

1. What were the characteristics of the ransomware attack on the viewpoint author's computer?
2. What factors kept the author from paying the ransom?
3. What has the author learned from his experiences?

We have all heard tales of cyber attacks, usernames and passwords stolen, databases infiltrated and corrupted. I did not fully appreciate the havoc such an attack could cause on

my legal practice and personal life until I became a victim of ransomware. Please take this article as a cautionary tale, with some tips to ensure you are protected or at least minimize damage from a cyber attack.

About a year ago I was working on my home computer when all of a sudden my computer started acting strangely. The screen shimmered, and then the background went black. As I tried to figure out what happened, I realized that all of my files (pdf, jpeg, MS Word, Excel, etc.) had been corrupted, and I no longer could access their contents. A window popped up on my screen notifying me that all my files had been encrypted and if I wanted the code to unencrypt the files, I would have to pay a $500 ransom with bitcoins. I was told I had five days to pay or the ransom would increase exponentially.

Over the course of ten minutes, the encryption spread throughout my entire personal computer and started to work its way through my online cloud storage program, which I use for my law practice. Fortunately, the cloud storage program I use automatically backs up all of my files multiple times throughout the day and could easily be restored. I had no such automated backup, however, on my personal home computer. Thus, I was completely cut off from thousands of pictures and personal documents. Many of these pictures were priceless to me.

I frantically called my IT specialist who rushed over and gave me the bad news that there was no way to recover the files unless I paid the ransom. In my mind, paying the $500 ransom was a small price to pay for recovering the priceless pictures of my son's childhood. I found myself, under the watchful eye of my IT specialist, searching the dark web to buy bitcoins. The closer I got to actually purchasing bitcoins, the more nervous I got. Several bitcoin sites wanted highly sensitive information such as my username and password for my personal bank accounts. Under no circumstance was I going to give up this information. Even if I paid the ransom, there was no guarantee the kidnappers would restore my files. There was a significant chance I would get repeatedly attacked with increasing ransom demands. I ultimately chose not to go forward with the extortion, and came to grips with the fact that many of my files would be lost forever.

My IT specialist purged my computer of all the infectious coding and encrypted files. He installed various programs to prohibit outside parties from rewriting my computer's coding, which is how the cyber attack occurred in the first place. We installed better antivirus software to automatically scan and remove threats. I also subscribed to an online cloud backup service, which automatically backs up the files on my computer every week.

What I have learned from this ordeal and what I would like to impart with the readers is the importance of being proactive. There are some pretty sophisticated and malicious criminal enterprises out there. Gone are the days where only reckless Internet surfers are at risk for such an attack. You have to be prepared.

Here are a few tips to ensure you are adequately protected:

- Do your research and select an effective antivirus software. I currently use Webroot and have had no complaints.
- Subscribe to a cloud-based backup service and make sure all of your devices and computers are automatically backing up your files. I currently use CrashPlan, and I periodically check to make sure everything is properly stored.

- Purchase an external hard drive and periodically backup all of your files so that you have a readily available and tangible source to restore lost files, preferably every week but no less than every month.
- If you use a cloud-based document storage or management system in your practice, make sure it has a restore function that allows you to restore your entire database to a specific event or date.

VIEWPOINT 4

Paying Off Ransomware Hackers Is an Individual Decision

Aarti Shahani

In the following viewpoint, Aarti Shahani argues that there are gray areas when it comes to ransomware, and there is no right or wrong way to respond to being a victim. Though most authorities on internet security will counsel clients not to pay a ransom, as it only encourages the creation of more malware, others are not so quick to issue a blanket statement. Because the encryption associated with ransomware is getting so sophisticated, it is virtually impossible to regain one's files without paying the ransom. It is up to the individual to weigh the cost of the ransom versus the inconvenience of losing perhaps many years of work. Aarti Shahani is a tech reporter on National Public Radio's (NPR) Business Desk. From her base in Silicon Valley, she covers the largest companies on Earth. In her reporting, Shahani works to pinpoint how economies and human relationships are being radically redefined by the tech sector.

As you read, consider the following questions:

1. How is ransomware different from other computer viruses?
2. What are some reasons for not paying the ransom?
3. What are some reasons for paying the ransom?

A lot of computer viruses hide inside your system. Hackers stealing your data go out of their way to operate quietly, stealthily, under the radar.

But there's another kind of attack that makes itself known—on purpose. It sneaks into your network and takes your files, holding them for ransom. It's called ransomware, and, according to cybersecurity experts, this kind of attack is getting more sophisticated.

Stick 'Em Up

Eric Young, who manages the computer network for a small business in Hermitage, Tenn., got a call from work. It was a Monday morning and, he says, it was "a very bad way to start the week."

Somebody in the office opened an email that looked legit. "It has the exact background of like PayPal," Young recalls, "and it says, somebody paid you money."

The employee clicked the link, and out popped a red alert that took up most of the screen. It was a threat: Pay ransom to an anonymous hacker, or all the files in the company network will be encrypted—locked up with a digital key that's so strong, no one can open them ever again.

The threat came with a countdown clock. Young had 72 hours and, as he tried to find solutions, the cyberthieves were slipping into every company computer—starting with Victim No. 1 and ending in the company's servers. "Our database was encrypted, and we were pretty much—we lost everything we had built for 14 years."

NPR spoke with other victims who did not want to be named for fear of losing their jobs or customers. But they described the same sequence of events.

One small business even called 911.

Lt. Catherine Buckley with the Colorado Springs Police Department reviews the call log for NPR.

The attack happened on Nov. 12. An officer went to the crime scene immediately. But when he got there, employees decided he couldn't really solve the problem. So they didn't file a police report. He left within 20 minutes.

Buckley reads from the department notes: "One of the employees had either received an email, or clicked on a link which opened up the malware CryptoWall 2.0."

The Tennessee company decided not to pay. It didn't trust the hackers to give back the files, so it relied on backups that it had. The Colorado Springs company did pay, in the amount of $750.

And here's where it gets weirder.

While ransomware criminals used to accept prepaid cards and other familiar forms of payment, they're now moving into so-called "cryptocurrency." Some rings only take Bitcoin, the electronic cash that's popular among hedge fund investors and online drug traders.

"[It is] not all that easy to come by," says Stu Sjouwerman, founder of the IT company KnowBe4. He keeps a Bitcoin wallet and has been paying ransom for small businesses hit by hackers. "That service is free," he says. "We meet perspective customers that way, and then tell them about our trainings and other services."

Ransomware Evolves

It's unclear how many people have been hit by ransomware. According to Rahul Kashyap, a researcher at the cybersecurity firm Bromium, the number is grossly underreported as victims feel shame and don't know where to turn for help.

"Many people might actually panic," he says. "They might believe that they did something wrong or they made a mistake which resulted in this compromise."

Bromium just released a study dissecting 30 cases of ransomware. It finds that the criminals are getting better at hiding their identities. Ransomware uses the anonymous online network Tor to conceal all communication between the attacker and victim. That way, for example, the CEO and IT support can't blame a specific employee, or help the employee.

Ransomware and the Internet of Things

The manufacturing industry is moving towards a connected world of Industry 4.0, which is the fourth industrial revolution where cyber-physical systems, Internet of Things and cloud computing bring automation and data driven efficiencies. There are benefits to be reaped through the use of Internet of Things. IoT devices can be anything from internet connected lights and valves on a gas pipe to toasters and fridges. These assets can have a digital identity which enables the owner to know the exact location, state and condition in real time. They can also be controlled remotely. The collection of all this data from multiple sources can allow a manufacturing plant to get a better insight into its workings, and control the small elements while seeing the bigger picture. Within a supply chain, it can give you visibility of parts and products that previously weren't available.

The flexibility that allows an authorised user access to this data and control can also potentially give an unauthorised user a backdoor. A backdoor that can be used to install a ransomware.

Some US hospitals are reported to have paid the ransom to get access to patient data. A recent freedom of data request found that the NHS has a good defence strategy. Of the 28 NHS trusts that were infected, none paid the ransom nor lost any data.

Now, IoT devices do not hold much data themselves for them to be worthwhile paying a ransom to unlock, but they do have access to real world systems; be that locks on the door or assets on the production line. This has a potential to do far more damage than just locking some data. The increased potential for damage also increases the financial risk for the asset owner and "potential" reward for the attacker. The attacker's success hangs on the cost of disruption being significantly greater than their asking price—the ransom amount.

There is no stopping the move towards Industry 4.0. Only by thinking about security now, can we truly benefit from the advances it brings… you know, instead of bunkering down after a breach.

"Industry 4.0 held to ransom – The destructive combination of IoT and ransomware," by Shahab Arif, hssmi.org, November 8, 2016.

"They wouldn't be able to block the victim from making the payment," Kashyap says. "So it works on both sides for the whole session to be anonymous."

The thieves are also getting better at finding valuable data. Just like gold is worth more than silver, a company's design for a high-rise building is worth more than a holiday memo. Hackers have written code to find high-end file extensions, "like autocad files used for designing industry structures."

Should You Pay?

The ransomware Cryptolocker was lucrative, with an estimated 500,000 victims targeted and $3 million in returns.

While the FBI managed to bust one ring based in Russia and Ukraine, Kashyap says, the problem isn't going away. New, stronger variants of Cryptolocker are already out.

But when asked if he advocates that victims pay the ransom, he says without pause, "Absolutely not. If you pay, they'll build more malware, pretty much as simple as that."

Security experts disagree on this point.

Jaeson Schultz at Cisco says a blanket policy is impractical: "Unless you've got powerful computers and a lot of time to spend guessing keys, there's really no way to get your data back unless you pay the ransom."

Chris Morales at NSS Labs says, "My mom owns her own company, and if it happened to her, I would tell her to pay."

The Department of Homeland Security tells people to not negotiate with the hackers. But another law enforcement agency, a sheriff's office in Tennessee, just paid to get its files back.

Ransomware has gotten so powerful, Morales says, the hackers really do lock down victims' data: "The truth is, is we have no way to recover their data if it gets destroyed. So we can't help them."

The very best defense, he says, is having a backup that's not connected to your machine in any way. Storing things on the cloud or on a USB drive that's plugged into your computer won't cut it.

Viewpoint 5

Hackers Are Refining Their Psychological Techniques in Order to Extort Money

Nova Safo

In the following viewpoint, Novo Safo argues that, as ransomware attacks become more common, the techniques that hackers use also gain sophistication. Hackers have learned to use increasingly clever psychological techniques in order to pressure or scare victims into paying the ransom. Official figures suggest the number of those who pay the ransom is very low, but unofficial figures may be much higher, as many people and organizations do not like to divulge that they've been scammed. Nova Safo is the Midwest correspondent for the global news service AFP, AgenceFrance-Presse, and was previously a reporter with the public radio economy and business news program Marketplace on National Public Radio and a correspondent for the now-defunct CNN Radio.

As you read, consider the following questions:

1. What is the irony concerning the encryption methods that hackers use?
2. How are hackers using psychology to coerce money from victims?
3. Why are so many people vulnerable to an attack?

A Los Angeles hospital has become the latest high-profile victim of a ransomware attack.

Hollywood Presbyterian Medical Center announced that it had paid $17,000 to hackers to regain control of its computer system. The hospital had been operating without it for 10 days.

Ransomware is a particularly pernicious hack. It is a type of hacker attack known as malware and can infect computers randomly through a visited website or directly target a person or organization through a well-crafted email. Hackers might have carefully researched social media accounts and relationships to ensure an email message—and an attached file—is opened.

Once ransomware enters a computer or computer system, it can either lock out users or encrypt files to make them unreadable without a digital key.

"Ransomware is basically an encryption program," said Bruce Schneier, a cybersecurity expert at Harvard's Berkman Center. "It breaks into your computer. It encrypts your files. And then it doesn't let you at them."

Because hackers are employing modern, highly sophisticated encryption, which ironically was designed to protect data, fighting a ransomware attack can be virtually impossible.

Hackers have also become increasingly sophisticated in hiding their identities. The L.A. hospital had to pay hackers in bitcoins, which are harder to trace.

That leaves many victims of ransomware in the same predicament: either to accept the loss of the data on their affected computers or to pay the hackers for the key to decrypt their files and restore access.

Cybersecurity experts say over the last several years, ransomware hackers have become increasingly sophisticated in using psychology and other methods to encourage victims to pay. For example, they design their ransom to be more palatable than the alternative.

"You want to ask for a number low enough that the victim will pay, and high enough to be profitable," Schneier said.

According to security firm Symantec, the average ransom was $300 and about 3 percent of victims paid. But because most pay quietly, Adam Kujawa, head of malware intelligence at the cybersecurity firm Malwarebytes, believes the number is a lot higher. Kujawa's firm provides security software to help detect malware attacks, including ransomware.

Kujawa said one of the reasons victims of malware choose not to disclose themselves is the sophisticated psychological techniques hackers employ. For example, they may falsely accuse victims of downloading child pornography on a locked-screen message that appears on a computer's display until a ransom is paid, Kujawa said.

The best recourse, according to cybersecurity experts, is to back up data. In the event of a ransomware attack, companies and individuals could then simply reformat their computers (scrubbing them clean) and reinstall data from backups.

"What we've always told people in the security community is do not pay the ransom. Never ever pay the ransom," Kujawa said. "But unfortunately some of these companies, and some of these users, have not employed backups. They have no way of getting the information back, other than just paying."

It's also important to update computer software, so that they are not susceptible to the latest known malware.

"People are not always as careful about protecting their machines as they could be ... or they don't run up-to-date antivirus," said Michael O'Reirdan, chairman emeritus of the Messaging, Malware and Mobile Anti-Abuse Working Group.

O'Reirdan said there are a lot of guesses as to how big the ransonmware problem has gotten, but because many companies and individuals don't report the attack, accurate statistics do not exist. Still, Symantec said it detected almost 9 million ransomware attacks in 2014, which was more than twice as many as the year before.

Periodical and Internet Sources Bibliography

The following articles have been selected to supplement the diverse views presented in this chapter.

Leonid Bershidsky, "The Russian Trail in the Latest 'Ransomware' Attack." *Bloomberg Quint*, June 30, 2017. https://www.bloombergquint.com/opinion/2017/06/29/the-russian-trail-in-the-latest-ransomware-attack.

Tim Culpan, "Global ransomware attacks ought to make Xi Jinping WannaSmile." *LiveMint*, May 16, 2017. http://www.livemint.com/Opinion/lkxIA4uGM2PdQLkMVyf7xH/Global-ransomware-attacks-ought-to-make-Xi-Jinping-WannaSmil.html.

Josh Fruhlinger, "The 5 biggest ransomware attacks of the last 5 years." *CSO*, August 1, 2017. https://www.csoonline.com/article/3212260/ransomware/the-5-biggest-ransomware-attacks-of-the-last-5-years.html.

The Japan Times, "The 'WannaCry' wake-up call." *Japan Times*, May 15, 2017. https://www.japantimes.co.jp/opinion/2017/05/15/editorials/wannacry-wake-call/.

Suman Layak, "Ransomware: The extortionists of the new millennium." *Economic Times*, May 21, 2017. https://economictimes.indiatimes.com/tech/internet/ransomware-the-extortionists-of-the-new-millennium/articleshow/58767354.cms.

Robert Lemos, "Recent ransomware attacks: Is it an epidemic or overblown?" *SearchSecurity*, October 2, 2017. http://searchsecurity.techtarget.com/feature/Recent-ransomware-attacks-Is-it-an-epidemic-or-overblown.

Nate Lord, "A History of Ransomware Attacks: The Biggest and Worst Ransomware Attacks of All Time." *DataInsider*, December 7, 2017. https://digitalguardian.com/blog/history-ransomware-attacks-biggest-and-worst-ransomware-attacks-all-time.

Fraser Moore, "Ransomware cyber-attacks by 'Russian hackers' could spark WORLD WAR 3, NATO chief warns." *Express*, June 29, 2017. https://www.express.co.uk/news/world/822570/world-war-three-ransomware-attack-hackers-nato-jens-stoltenberg.

David Strom, "The rise of ransomware." *Hewlett Packard Enterprise*, September 10, 2017. https://www.hpe.com/us/en/insights/articles/the-rise-of-ransomware-1709.html.

Chapter 4

Combatting Cyberterrorism and Ransomware

Viewpoint 1

Countries Should Cooperate to Counter Cyberterrorism

Shavit Matias

In the following viewpoint, Shavit Matias argues that given North Korea's attack on Sony Pictures, as well as news from around the world, cyberterrorism is becoming an unfortunate reality. The author discusses the various measures that countries from Iran to England are taking to beef up their internet security and, in many cases, their cyber attack capabilities. Matia believes that it is the countries that are not currently invested in controlling their cyberspace domain that are most vulnerable to a cyberterrorist attack. Therefore, she argues, countries across the world need to cooperate with each other in order to ward off disaster. Shavit Matias is an international law and globalization expert. She was the first Deputy Attorney General of Israel for International Law, and is a Research Fellow at the Hoover Institution at Stanford University.

As you read, consider the following questions:

1. According to Fox News, how are terrorists attempting to advance their cyberterrorism capabilities?
2. How are various countries worldwide attempting to meet the cyber challenge?
3. What does the author recommend that all countries should do to be better prepared for a cyber-threat?

"Combating Cyberattacks in the Age of Globalization," by Shavit Matias, Board of Trustees of Leland Stanford Junior University, March 5, 2015. Reprinted by permission.

The cyberattack late last year on Sony Pictures, intended to deter the release of the movie "The Interview"—combined with threats of physical harm to civilians—threw once again into sharp relief the complexity and dangers of cyberspace. As the heated exchanges between Washington and Pyongyang continue, the weaknesses in cyber defense of private companies and states is again evident, not only in repelling the attack, but in identifying the hackers as well.

The Sony attack is far from a solitary occurrence. Beyond the already well-known cybercrime and cyber espionage phenomena, a dangerous and complex realm is emerging where the level of sophistication of terror groups and states is growing. Cyberterrorism and cyberwarfare have become a key national security threat.

By way of some examples, in September 2014, various news outlets reported that jihadists in the Middle East, including leaders from both the Islamic State (also known as ISIS) and al Qaeda, were actively planning cyberterror attacks against Western countries, specifically targeting government servers and critical infrastructure. It was further reported that ISIS was planning to establish a "cyber caliphate" "intending to mount catastrophic hacking and virus attacks on America and the West." According to Fox News,

> ...the terror groups are trying to add to their numbers to boost their capabilities, using social media to reach a larger pool of potential recruits and calling on militant-minded specialists to join them. The targets are the websites of US government agencies, banks, energy companies and transport systems. Islamic State's efforts are spearheaded by a British hacker known as Abu Hussain al Britani, whose real name is Junaid Hussein. He fled his hometown of Birmingham for Syria a year ago to join the group and US intelligence sources say he is one of several key recruiters. Al Britani once led a group of teenage British hackers called Team Poison, and now actively calls for computer-literate jihadists to come to Syria and Iraq.

Iran and North Korea are heavily investing in cyberwarfare capabilities, building as part of their military establishment sophisticated cyber units with defensive and offensive capabilities. A 22-page analysis of Iranian cyberwarfare capabilities published in August by Israel's Institute for National Security Studies concludes that during the course of 2013, Iran became one of the key players in the international cyberwarfare theater, and points to the many major qualitative and quantitative investments by Iran in this field. The paper outlines cyberattacks conducted by Iran, including a relatively recent large-scale attack on the websites of key banks and financial institutions in the United States, stating that "information security experts described this attack as 'unprecedented in scope and effectiveness.'" Israel has also attributed to Iran numerous cyberattack attempts.

A July 7, 2014 article in Security Affairs reports that North Korea doubled the number of units of its cyber army (now estimated to employ approximately 6,000 people), has established overseas bases for hacking attacks, and "is massive[ly] training its young prodigies to become professional hackers." According to the article, "the North Korean cyber army has already hit many times the infrastructure of South Korea, banks, military entities, media and TV broadcasters with malware and other sophisticated techniques."

Russia and China have also heavily invested in such capabilities, and it is reported that their specialized cyberwarfare units are behind several instances of network disruption, technology theft and other cyberattacks against governments and companies. On February 4, 2014, the website tripwire.com reported that "Russian government officials have announced they intend to create a designated military unit devoted to preventing cyber-based attacks from disrupting vital systems devoted to Russian military operations" and that the new unit is expected to be fully operational by 2017.

In March of 2014 it was reported that the Latvian army had hired the country's first 13 cyber guards as part of a newly created cyber defense unit.

In a 2012 speech on cybersecurity, then-FBI Director Robert Mueller stated that: "Terrorism remains the FBI's top priority. But in the not-too-distant future, we anticipate that the cyber threat will pose the number one threat to our country." Former US Secretary of Defense Leon Panetta and former director of the NSA Keith Alexander have repeatedly warned against a future "cyber Pearl Harbor."

Similarly, the US Department of Defense's 2014 Quadrennial Defense Review declares:

> The Joint Force must also be prepared to battle increasingly sophisticated adversaries who could employ advanced warfighting capabilities while simultaneously attempting to deny US forces the advantages they currently enjoy in space and cyberspace. We will sustain priority investments in science, technology, research, and development both within the defense sector and beyond. [...] Innovation is paramount given the increasingly complex warfighting environment we expect to encounter.

Over the past decade, facing the alarming growth of cyberattacks on industry, media, banks, infrastructure and state institutions, there has been an increasing focus of industry and states on building tools to enhance capabilities to combat cybercrime, cyber espionage, cyberterrorism and cyberwarfare, and there is a major shift of funds, efforts, and focus to these areas. Many countries are creating cyber defense institutions within their national security establishments and enhancing their cyber capabilities, including through the creation of dedicated cyberwarfare units within their defense forces. Others are beginning to be aware of the necessity. According to Director of National Intelligence James R. Clapper in a January 29, 2014 Statement for the Record before the Senate Select Committee on Intelligence, the United States estimates that several of the cyber defense institutions created by states will likely be responsible for offensive cyber operations as well.

The cyber arena is complex and continuously evolving. Recognizing the critical interlink between the various actors and the need for cooperation and innovation, states are increasingly trying to build cooperation between domestic state cyber institutions and industry and academia, and devise mechanisms for internal cooperation between different state units and agencies. While in the past states kept many of these efforts—including information on the formation of military cyber units—relatively secret, today they increasingly publicize their efforts both nationally and internationally.

"Be an Army hacker: This top secret cyber unit wants you" shouts the headline of an April 6, 2013 article in the *Military Times*, explaining that the US Army is looking for computer-savvy American troops to "turn into crack cyberwarriors" for both offensive and defensive purposes. The United States Cyber Command has already announced that over the next few years it intends to recruit 6,000 cyber experts and create teams of soldiers and civilians to assist the Pentagon in defending US national infrastructure.

The United Kingdom is also going public with its efforts. A new cyber unit called the Joint Cyber Reserve has been set up by the Ministry of Defence to help protect critical computer networks from attack, and former Defence Secretary Philip Hammond appealed to Britain's top IT experts to join up and work as military reservists.

Israel has been at the forefront of building defenses from cyberattacks—and it too has gone public with its establishment of cyberwarfare units. According to a November 14, 2013 article in the Israeli newspaper *Haaretz*, the Israeli military has been "bullish" on the cyber front—not only creating sophisticated cyber units but actively involved in "raising the next generation of cyber geeks" through after-school programs and other initiatives geared at preparing today's youth to fight this new kind of war. This is in addition to the establishment of a new national cyber defense authority in conjunction with the Israeli National Cyber Bureau.

As early as 2011, a study on cybersecurity and cyberwarfare conducted by the Center for Strategic and International Studies (CSIS) had already identified 33 states that include cyberwarfare

Governments Must Hire Tech Wizards

There's a wonderful Amy Schumer sketch in which the comedian takes her mother and her laptop along to a therapist to try to address the anger that Schumer feels when confronted with her mum's computer incompetence. "Let's attach the photo," Schumer says, once her mum has managed to switch the machine on. "To the computer?" Schumer closes her eyes, frustrated: "No. To the email." "Well," her mum says, disheartened, "I didn't bring a cord."

It's a keenly observed study that those of us who are young, or relatively young, know all too well when it comes to parents and technology. It is less amusing when it isn't one's mum who's not 100% sure what the shift key is for, or that the "internet" and the "web" aren't interchangeable, but the people with responsibility for the smooth running of our country.

Which brings us to the NHS ransomware attack, or "ranzomware attack." Not to be a secondary school teacher about this, but failing to prepare is preparing to fail, and that is exactly what happened with this attack. Ministers made the decision to end the NHS contract with Microsoft back in 2010, while many trusts were still using an old operating system (Windows XP). When operating systems become defunct, as newer versions are rolled out, eventually the maker stops supporting them and providing fixes, or "patches," for their vulnerabilities. This isn't even technological knowledge, it is simple market economics.

The government made the decision not to extend the deal, but instead pay £5.5m for support from Microsoft for the old operating systems. That deal ended a year ago and hospital trusts were advised to move to a more up-to-date system, which would have the latest security updates. Perhaps if health secretary Jeremy Hunt understood tech better—he says he does—last week's ransomware attack might have been averted. Updating systems would not have been a choice for trusts, but something mandated by central government.

Trust chief executives must take more interest in tech and NHS Digital should do a better job of making sure they spend on cybersecurity; some spend nothing at all. Nobody is saying that the NHS IT system is going to be as easy to maintain as switching it on and off again, but that's precisely why the government needs to start taking tech seriously and investing in those who understand it.

"To prevent more cyberattacks, we need real tech experts in government," by Hannah Jane Parkinson, Guardian News and Media Limited.

in their military planning and organization. According to the report, "Common elements in military doctrine include the use of cyber capabilities for reconnaissance, information operations, the disruption of critical networks and services, for 'cyberattacks,' and as a complement to electronic warfare and information operations. Some states include specific plans for informational and political operations. Others link cyberwarfare capabilities with existing electronic warfare planning." The report also points out that in another 36 states, civilian agencies charged with internal security missions, computer security, or law enforcement are also responsible for cybersecurity.

The cutting edge for military organizations, the CSIS report explains, is the creation of specific commands dedicated to cyberwarfare, similar to the United States Cyber Command created in 2009. At the time of the 2011 study, CSIS found that 12 states—including North Korea, Denmark, Germany, India, Iran, and South Korea—had established or were planning to establish similar commands. It is likely that other states, such as Cuba and the Russian Federation, will or are developing such organizations as well.

So the cyber swords are sharpened and drawn and have indeed already struck. Western countries spend substantial funds to train and employ many personnel in military establishments, defense establishments, universities, industry, and elsewhere to defend against cybercrime, cyberterrorism, cyberwarfare, and industry attacks, as well as building up their offensive capabilities.

Importantly, and as an additional challenge, these states will have to devise the correct balance between the need to confront these cyber phenomena and the privacy rights of citizens, as the United States has discovered in the wake of the Snowden affair. States that have until now taken a very strict view of privacy, particularly in the European Union, are now coping with difficult privacy questions in light of an increasing amount of terrorist attacks and a new phenomenon where it is has been estimated that 5,000 of their own young citizens have joined ISIS, which itself uses cyberspace and social media heavily to recruit as well as to make public their deadly activities. These European recruits may be operating against their home states, and may return to Europe and conduct terrorist attacks there, yet until recently they were undetected.

The threat is real and omnipresent. While some states are well into building up their capabilities, others are beginning, and there are those that have not even begun.

But whatever stage of preparation a state is in, given the realities of the age of globalization, it is unlikely the solution to national security cyber threats will be found by states trying to act on their own, no matter how sophisticated their internal mechanisms, protections, or armies may be. As states are grappling with their own internal organization, their legal questions (under both domestic and international law), and building their capabilities, they must also look—much sooner than later—to the international front and the challenges it poses to their national security interests.

Cyberterrorism, cyberwarfare and cybercrime are globalized phenomena cutting at light speed across borders, and are committed by attackers who are often difficult to locate and even sometimes impossible to identify. Combating the cyber criminals and terrorists, as well as cyber military units, will require not only strong domestic infrastructure and capabilities, but also similarly strong capabilities and infrastructure in other like-minded states and robust cooperation mechanisms between states and their various institutions, intelligence agencies, and militaries. Cybercrime, cyberwarfare and cyberterrorism can hit national security as well as other interests of a state from places where, without international cooperation, a state has little or no control, nor will it have, without international cooperation, sufficient ability to defend or protect itself.

Furthermore, globalization, and the link between countries and economies, creates many national security interests well beyond state borders. A major attack on the critical infrastructure or military operations of a NATO state in a way that falls under NATO Article 5 is one example. A major attack on offshore branches of US companies or banks in a way that will critically affect the US economy, or an electronic takeover of air command of airports in different areas of the world are others. The scenarios are almost unlimited.

It is not unlikely that the terrorists or states wanting to attack a particular state or business using cyberterrorism or cyberwarfare will look for the weakest links in the global chain, and hit wherever they can to harm their primary target.

The creation of a global action strategic plan in that regard must be a priority. International standards and norms—including enforcement mechanisms—to be applied across the board by states, and mechanisms for information sharing and cooperation, must be put in place sooner rather than later.

While there have been some efforts in different international forums to address the issue—for example, various UN groups of government experts have been convening over the last few years in an effort to achieve consensus and common understandings on the norms that apply with respect to cybersecurity—to date these efforts have had limited impact. Many times, debates on form supplant debates on substance, and progress, if made, is slow. NATO members are making some moves in a cooperative direction, whether in building some capabilities for cooperation between NATO members or examining the relevant international law with the assistance of the impressive Tallinn manual, and there are some efforts in assisting weaker states to strengthen their capabilities, but this too is only a first step.

In order to address the mounting cyber challenges ahead, weaker states, whether NATO members or not, will need assistance in building up their capabilities. Domestic standards, laws, and institutions for combating cybercrime, cyberterrorism and cyberwarfare will need to be put in place. International legal parameters will need to be defined and significant mechanisms for information sharing and cooperation will need to be created.

This will not be an easy venture. There is and will likely be much political and other opposition from states, as well as concerns over information sharing. The challenge is all the more daunting in light of the diametrically opposed views of the United States and other Western countries, on the one hand, and Russia and China on the other, regarding the manner in which cyberspace should be regulated. But while states are struggling with legal and other definitions, and debating their differences, terror organizations are forging right ahead as are unfriendly cyber armies. Time is not on the side of the Western nations, nor is it on the side of their private domestic industry and businesses that are many times the targets of the cyberattacks.

A concentrated effort is needed to try to close this serious gap in security. Lessons learnt from other international efforts—such as mechanisms and standards put in place to combat terrorism, money laundering, organized crime, trafficking in persons, or corruption—can be examined and, where applicable, could perhaps be followed and expanded and elaborated upon to meet the different needs arising from the serious and dangerous cyber challenge. Although devising international instruments and mechanisms for the cyber threat is likely much more complex, for a range of reasons, these examples interlinking trade interests, blacklists, sanctions, diplomatic pressure, and other measures with the creation of domestic and international standards and instruments have assisted to an extent in combating these cross-border phenomena.

These examples, which include also the creation of certain mechanisms for cooperation and information sharing, standards for industry, as well as other standards, show that in the age of globalization not only is it necessary to create the norms and infrastructure for states to work together to combat cross-border issues, but it may also be more possible to persuade states to do so if a strong lead is taken, whether by one powerful state or a group of states. Compelling measures must be put in place making it in the direct interests of states and industry to cooperate and adopt standards and cooperation methodologies.

Cyberterrorism, cybercrime and cyberwarfare pose a real and significant threat to national security. Together with increasing domestic efforts, it is time for strong operation on the international front.

Viewpoint 2

Hackers Target Computers with Outdated Operating Systems

Simon Parkinson

In the following viewpoint Simon Parkinson argues that ransomware and other malware takes aim at computers that have not been updated with current operating systems. Microsoft, the maker of Windows, has moved on to newer systems such as Windows 10 and does not support the very popular old system, Windows XP, with updates any longer. This makes XP vulnerable to attack. In the wake of such ransomware attacks as WannaCry, organizations often put forth the money need to upgrade systems, but it is better to do so preventatively, before an attack. Simon Parkinson is Senior Lecturer in Informatics within the school of Computing and Engineering at the University of Huddersfield in the United Kingdom.

As you read, consider the following questions:

1. Why do old operating systems, such as Windows XP, place those using them at risk?
2. Why do many organizations not upgrade to newer, safer operating systems?
3. Why are private sector corporations even more at risk than public ones?

Hospitals across Britain were crippled by the recent ransomware cyber-attack, making the country's National Health Service one of the most high-profile victims of the global incident.

The government has been criticised for cutting IT support for the health service and failing to replace old computer systems. Meanwhile, ministers hit out at NHS bosses for not improving cybersecurity, amid reports that an upgrade that could have prevented the attack was made available a month ago.

This story doesn't feel too surprising. Anyone who regularly deals with public services in person will probably have seen government employees struggling with outdated computer systems. Certainly, other major state-run organisations have also been hit by the ransomware, including German railway company Deutsche Bahn and the US Department of Homeland Security. But is the public sector really any worse than the private sector at keeping its IT security up to date and avoiding cybercrime?

The recent "WannaCry" attack was made possible by a flaw in the 15-year-old Windows XP operating system. Software manufacturers often provide updates or patches to their products after they discover such a flaw, to prevent cyber-criminals from exploiting it. However, Microsoft stopped routinely updating XP in 2014, and those still using it have to pay for custom support to receive any further patches.

Once the company became aware of the WannaCry flaw, it was quick to release a patch back in March. But because many customers were still using unsupported versions of XP, WannaCry rapidly infected a large number of systems when it emerged in May. Microsoft then made its patch available to all XP users but many of those who didn't update immediately were caught out. This is exactly what happened within the NHS.

The government has long acknowledged the need to update its old IT systems. When public XP support ended in 2014, the government said it expected the majority of its machines to be upgraded within a year. It then ended NHS funding for custom XP support, reportedly in an attempt to encourage health service bosses to upgrade their systems. But a report at the end of 2016 suggested that 90% of NHS trusts still had at least one XP system.

The most likely reason that out-of-date systems are still being used is the cost of upgrading them. In most cases, a new version of Windows or another operating system would also need a new computer that was powerful enough to run it, and potentially new bespoke hardware and software to enable the organisation to do its job. For example, a hospital X-ray department using an XP-based machine might need a new version of the software that controls its X-ray machines.

Public sector agencies also have a luxury in the form of highly-skilled government experts from the likes of the National Cyber Security Centre who are available to ensure that critical services, such as the NHS, are kept operational. So even if the recent ransomware attack acts as a necessary wake-up call, there's still a perceived safety net.

Private Problem

However, WannaCry didn't just affect the public sector. Around 200,000 victims in 150 countries have been affected, according to EU police force Europol, many of them businesses including major corporations such as Nissan, FedEx and Hitachi. One source suggests that more than 10% of all desktop PCs run Windows XP, and a significant portion of those victims will likely be small businesses. In general, there is no specific evidence that public sector organisations suffer cyber-attacks disproportionately.

Although the NHS is clearly under tight financial constraints, governments have significant resources to mitigate cyber-threats and can raise large amounts of money if politicians choose to do so. In the UK, the National Cyber Security Centre alone has a £1.9 billion investment.

It is a completely different picture for small companies that don't have easy access to cash for upgrades or access to the highly-skilled resources of government experts or even IT departments. Often they don't even have the awareness that there's a problem

Governments and Cyberattacks

Cyber-attacks are on the rise and everyone and everything from celebrities to hospitals are being targeted.

Some are expecting government to take the lead on next steps, but earlier this year, a cyber-security risk analysis firm scored US local, state and federal governments at the bottom of a ranking comparing 17 private industries such as healthcare and retail.

The report, by security rating startup SecurityScorecard, took in 600 government organizations and said they struggled in particular with malware infections, network security and software patching.

"Federal agencies may be susceptible to more risk due to the sheer size of their infrastructure, but in many cases, may be prepared to fare better against cyber-security threats due to larger budgets and teams of security personnel," SecurityScorecard analysts wrote.

As an advisor to the Japanese government, I see these sorts of problems all too often—both inside Japan as well as outside when talking with colleagues overseas, including regularly at World Economic Forum gatherings.

Governments are in many cases sluggish instead of nimble when dealing with cyber threats. But they have also realized that stopping cyber threats is a balancing act: too many overprotective laws and regulations and the productivity gained from online activities and the use of ICT slows to a crawl. Government size is often a handicap but, as the report notes, IT budgets can be secured to deal with cyber-security. That's why it's hard to be sympathetic when the public sector gets hacked.

One thing I've preached time and time again is the need for various ministries and agencies in government to coordinate strategy and resources when fighting cyber-attacks. The interconnectedness and interdependence of today's world means that a threat to one part of government is a threat to the whole.

"This is what makes governments vulnerable to hackers," by William H. Saito, World Economic Forum, August 22, 2016.

to begin with. There are government-backed initiatives to help small companies with cybersecurity, such as the UK's Cyber Essentials, but these don't have the scale to reach everyone or even identify and help those most in need. We can certainly question whether they are having much impact given the scale of the recent Ransomware attack.

Cyber-attacks on the scale of WannaCry may remind organisations about the need to maintain their IT security. Getting people to understand how is still a serious challenge. Public sector organisations might too often rely on outdated computer systems but at least they're better placed than much of the private sector to do something about it.

Today's Cars Are Vulnerable Targets for Cyberterrorism

Cheryl Dancey Balough and Richard C. Balough

Today's automobiles are computer systems on wheels. They are subject to cyberattack and cyberterrorism, and will be more so in the future. Hackers might be able to take control of a vehicle through numerous cyber entry points in a car's system. The legalities of such a situation are complex. It is an open question whether automobile companies should be held responsible for attacks on their products that may injure or kill drivers and riders. Both auto manufacturers and legislators must take action to deal with the complexities of this issue. Cheryl Dancey Balough and Richard C. Balough are attorneys in Chicago. Cheryl Dancey Balough is the communications co-director of the American Bar Association's Cyberspace Law Committee and adjunct professor at Chicago-Kent College of Law. Richard C. Balough is the co-chair of the American Bar Association's Mobile Commerce Subcommittee of the Cyberspace Law Committee.

As you read, consider the following questions:

1. What factors make computerized automobiles subject to cyber attack?
2. What techniques can hackers use to gain access to cars?
3. Will automobile companies be held liable for damage incurred as a result of cyberterrorism?

Today's cars are controlled by complex computer systems that include millions of lines of code connected by internal networks. Cars have become computers on wheels. The potential exists that a car's computers, like any computer system, can be hacked, leaving the car vulnerable to infection by malware. These vulnerabilities pose serious safety hazards should they be exploited nefariously. Legal implications of this technological vulnerability have yet to be adequately addressed.

Multiple Points of Entry into a Car's Computer Systems

Cars have dozens of electronic control units (ECUs) embedded in the body, doors, dash, roof, trunk, seats, wheels, navigation equipment, and entertainment centers. Common wired networks interconnect these ECUs, which also can connect to the Internet. This architecture provides almost unlimited gateways for external hacking and infection with malware. Some entry points to a car's ECUs require a direct, hard-wired connection, while others can be accessed wirelessly, including using Wi-Fi or RFID. Once entry is gained, a hacker can take over all of a car's computer-controlled systems.

In Austin, Texas, a disgruntled former employee of an auto dealer hacked into the dealer's computer system and remotely activated the vehicle immobilization system, triggering the horn and disabling the ignition system in more than 100 vehicles. This anti-theft system had been installed by the dealer as a method of addressing non-payment by customers. While the anti-theft device was connected to the car's horn and ignition, the hacker did not take further control of the car.

Direct Entry via the OBD-II Port

All cars made after 1996 are required to have an Onboard Diagnostics connection (OBD-II) located within two feet of the steering wheel. All cars manufactured after 2008 must share the same OBD-II protocol. The OBD-II's initial function was to monitor mandated emissions equipment. Today, the port is used to monitor and control multiple functions. Service personnel plug equipment into the port for both diagnostics and ECU programming, typically via Windows-based computers, creating at least two paths for the introduction of malware.

First, dealership computers typically connect to the Internet (and often are required by manufacturers to do so) for daily program updates. During that process, malware could be downloaded, infecting the computers. They in turn could spread the malware when connected to a car's OBD-II port. A second pathway is hacking into the dealership's internal wireless network. One university research team found that it was thereby possible to use the dealer's Wi-Fi to mount an attack.

More than dealers and mechanics use the OBD-II port. Parents can connect an app to the port to remotely monitor their children's driving, and fleet managers use apps to keep tabs on how their fleet vehicles are being driven. In addition to hackers intent on introducing malware, clever thieves can access the port to clone "smart keys" and simply drive away with a stolen car.

Remote Entry Points

The federal government also mandates that a car have an event data recorder (EDR), similar to an airplane's black box to record data about the status and operation of a car's systems. While historically EDR information was collected only via physical download, primarily to conduct a post-crash assessment, newer EDR systems permit data collection over remote wireless networks. The systems automatically transmit information to an emergency response center when an accident occurs. If the EDR can communicate via a wireless network to a data collection center, then malware similarly could be transmitted back to infect the EDR.

Entertainment systems, hands-free cellphone operations, and satellite radio also provide access points to introduce malware into a car's ECUs. For example, malware could be included in a CD inserted into the car's entertainment system. If an attacker can compromise a smartphone that uses a car's Bluetooth, the attacker can leverage the smartphone to compromise the car's telematics unit. Other paths to a car's ECUs can be accessed only at short range, such as remote keyless entry. Even tire pressure monitoring systems, which use wireless communication, are vulnerable and thus can open a pathway to the entire car's systems.

Car manufacturers are rushing to add new Wi-Fi functions as selling points. General Motors announced that for 2014 it will offer 4G LTE wireless, allowing passengers to access a Wi-Fi hot spot for use by multiple portable devices like phones and laptops. In the past two decades, car manufacturers have begun offering remote telematics systems on their vehicles, such as General Motors' OnStar, Toyota's SafetyConnect, and Ford's Sync. These systems use mobile phone voice and data communication, in conjunction with GPS technology, to give drivers hands-free remote access to emergency services, vehicle diagnostics, directions, and e-mail access. These services continue to evolve and now enable security measures such as remote ignition block and remote deceleration of a stolen vehicle. Computer scientists have demonstrated the ability to hack into such cellular-based telematics systems, transmit commands to vehicles, and surreptitiously listen to interior vehicle conversations.

Total Access All of the Car's Computer Systems

Because all of the car's ECUs are interconnected, once an entry point is found via any ECU, a hacker can access all car systems. While the Austin, Texas, incident demonstrates the vulnerability of a car's computer systems in a relatively benign way, not all hackers will be so restrained. Computer scientists at the University of California, San Diego, and the University of Washington conducted multiple experiments using various remote access modalities. For every vulnerability demonstrated, they could take complete control of a vehicle's systems—both while at rest and when traveling at high speeds. In addition, by hacking a car's computer, a thief could remotely unlock a car's doors, turn on its engine, arrive at the car's location, and drive off.

Even more menacing is automobile cyberterrorism, through which a terrorist could control cars via malware, using many of the same techniques for hacking into regular computers. This vulnerability could create mayhem on the roads if a hacker broke into a vehicle network and "ordered" car ignitions to turn off or brakes to engage or disengage. In 2010, the United States and Israel allegedly created the Stuxnet worm, which reportedly destroyed 1,000 centrifuges Iran used to enrich uranium by taking over the computerized systems operating the centrifuges. Stuxnet alerted critical infrastructure providers to the lack of protection from basic hacking. Automakers are no different than other infrastructure providers and are similarly vulnerable to cyberterrorism.

V2V and Self-Driving Cars

The potential vulnerability of cars to hacking will increase as vehicle-to-vehicle (V2V) and self-driving cars become available. V2V communication allows vehicles to send each other via Wi-Fi information such as location, speed, and direction of travel. Other data that may be exchanged include lateral acceleration, longitudinal acceleration, throttle position, brake status, steering angle, headline status, and the number of occupants in the vehicle.

Companies are gearing up for the V2V market. Google has been testing cars controlled solely by computers. Ford Motor Company expects to launch such cars by 2017. Two states, Nevada and California, have passed legislation allowing driverless cars on their roads. It is estimated that by 2040, self-driving cars could account for 75 percent of road traffic. At the 2013 Detroit Auto Show, Audi demonstrated a self-parking car, which one can retrieve from the garage via smartphone.

Industry and Government Addressing the Threat

One security expert estimates that the average auto maker is about 20 years behind software companies in understanding how to prevent cyberattacks. Like many computer systems, car computers previously were "air-gapped" from the Internet but are now connected via cell phones, Bluetooth, computerized diagnostic systems, and other exposed entry points. As long as the ECUs were not connected externally, the danger of introducing malware into a car was low and, as a result, the need to have sophisticated and updated security controls remained a low priority. Given today's connections, however, control systems must be designed to thwart cyberattacks.

This very real threat has prompted both the auto industry and the government to begin taking action. General Motors has a patent application pending for remote reprogramming of vehicle flash memory using digital satellite broadcast or other wireless transmission to the vehicle, thereby closing any "air-gap" between the car's ECUs and the Internet or any potential cyberattacker. SAE International, North America's largest automotive trade group, formed a special committee to draft new standards for security measures in automotive electronic systems. The US Department of Transportation also is revising its testing procedures for automotive electronics.

Until industry-wide standards are adopted and implemented, cars, their owners, and their passengers remain vulnerable, creating liability concerns for the automotive industry. If a malware attack were to occur, vehicle owners might be able to assert causes of action for defective design under state laws and for breach of implied warranty pursuant to the federal Magnuson-Moss Act. Most states have consumer protection laws targeted at unfair methods of competition and unfair or deceptive practices. These statutes might create a duty to disclose an objective, identifiable safety risk to consumers. California courts have found that defects in automobiles that could cause sudden or unexpected engine failure while driving pose such a risk. Evidence that a defect causes car engines to shut off unexpectedly or causes individuals to stop their cars under dangerous conditions also can trigger the duty to disclose.

In a class action involving plastic coolant tubes that cracked, leaked, or otherwise failed in a car, the plaintiffs alleged that the defendants knew, reasonably should have known, or were reckless in not knowing about the coolant tube defect but failed to disclose the defect to consumers. The court found the allegations were sufficient to sustain causes of action under many state consumer protection acts. The court also found that the Magnuson-Moss Act claims required that the warranties be determined by state law, and the court conducted a state-by-state analysis, finding the allegations sufficient in some states but deficient in others.

Similarly, if a court were to find that an auto maker knew or should have known about its cars' vulnerability to hacking and should have disclosed that vulnerability, then a consumer might have a cause of action under consumer protection laws. As for a breach of implied warranty claim, cars generally have warranties expressed in a number of years or miles. There is no specific "shrink wrap" type of agreement for the millions of lines of code in today's cars. If a court were to find an implied warranty that runs with a car's ECUs, then this cause of action might also exist for consumers if their cars are hacked into and controlled by malware.

Consumers whose car ECUs are compromised might alternatively sue auto makers under a defective design theory. Toyota owners took this approach after their vehicles suddenly accelerated. The court denied Toyota's motion to dismiss finding the complaint supported a design-defect claim given that the cars "do not meet consumer expectation because they suddenly and unexpectedly accelerate and cannot be stopped upon proper application of the brake pedal, [causing] crash and injuries." The court also denied Toyota's motion to dismiss a count for "warning defect theory," which allows for a cause of action even though a product is manufactured or designed flawlessly if the manufacturer later learns there is a product defect.

While auto companies may argue that the threat of a third party inserting malware into a car and taking it over is beyond their control because it is external, similar arguments in the past have been rejected. Otherwise, courts have noted, all defective designs would be characterized as external even if they are predictable.

Similarly, in the case of a malware invasion through inadequately protected points of entry to a car's systems, the threat is not just external, but predictable. By failing to protect the car's systems from malware, the predictable consequences are potentially disastrous and car companies might be liable for defective design of the computer systems without adequate protection in light of known cyber threats.

Protected Computer Under the CFAA?

Even with the efforts of multiple groups to thwart automobile cyberterrorism and other malicious attacks on car computer systems, the past couple of decades have taught us that hackers will always try to stay a step ahead. It is important to determine whether existing laws provide viable means to address hacking into automotive computer systems as a civil cause of action or criminal offense.

If a hacker or terrorist gains access to a car's ECUs and installs malware, that insertion would be without authorization under the Computer Fraud and Abuse Act (CFAA). The ECUs meet the CFAA's definition of a "computer," that is, the ECUs are high speed data processing devices performing logical, arithmetic, or storage functions. More problematic, however, is whether a car and its ECUs meet the definition of a CFAA "protected computer." In order to qualify, the car or ECU must be a computer "which is used in or affecting interstate or foreign commerce. . . ." Cars do travel in interstate commerce, but does the computer system affect interstate commerce as defined under the CFAA? At least one court found that in order to qualify as a protected computer, a computer must be used in interstate commerce. In other words, if the computing activity at issue takes place entirely within one state, the computers are not used in interstate commerce.

Even if a car itself is not a protected computer, the pathway to hacking a car's ECUs might involve a protected computer. If a person takes a car to a dealership for routine maintenance, a dealer's infected diagnostic computer could introduce malware into the car through its OBD-II port. Because the dealer's computer connects to the Internet, it is a protected computer under the CFAA. Similarly, a person may subscribe to an auto insurance company's program that monitors car usage to reduce premiums. The insurer tracks the car's usage in part by attaching a monitoring device to the OBD-II port. If the insurer's computers are hacked to plant malware aimed at cars, this malware could be transferred in violation of the CFAA when the insurer's computer connects to the insured's car—a use in interstate commerce.

Whether or not the CFAA applies, car dealerships and insurance companies need to determine how they will address hacking. If a dealership or insurer discovers its computer system has been compromised to the point of infecting car ECUs, disclosure of the incident might not be mandated under state laws because the breach does not involve personal information. Given liability concerns, however, disclosing the security breach to car owners might be wise.

The DMCA and Protection

Assuming some software programs used to operate a car's systems are copyrighted and automakers have taken measures to prevent access, hacking into a car might violate the Digital Millennium Copyright Act (DMCA), which prohibits circumvention of technological measures to gain access to a copyrighted work. The DMCA's anti-circumvention provision creates a separate cause of action even when no copyright infringement exists. The Ninth Circuit found a violation of this provision in *MDY Industries, LLC v. Blizzard Entertainment Inc.*, 629 F.3d 928 (9th Cir. 2010). However, the appellate court declined to grant the plaintiff relief because the technology used to prevent access was not an effective access control measure. In reaching its decision, the appellate court cited a Sixth Circuit case, which found that to qualify under the DMCA, the technological measure must effectively prevent access. Therefore, a party seeking to use the DMCA to pursue the hacker of a car's ECUs would need to show that its car has technological measures that effectively control access.

Possible Violation of the Wiretap Act

Hacking into a car's ECUs might not by itself be a violation the Wiretap Act, but how a hacker inserts malware into a car's ECUs could violate the act. The Wiretap Act prohibits intentional interception of an "electronic communication," which it defines as "any transfer of signs, signals, writing, images, sounds, data, or intelligence of any nature transmitted in whole or in part by a wire, radio, electromagnetic, photoelectronic or photooptical system that affects interstate or foreign commerce." 18 U.S.C. § 2510(12). A hacker's interception of signals or data transmission between the ECUs within a car arguably would not affect interstate commerce. In addition, insertion of malware into a car's internal networks through its OBD-II port, a DVD, or a USB drive connected to a mechanic's diagnostic system without interception of data would not implicate the Wiretap Act because no interception occurs. However, if a hacker actually intercepts an electronic transmission, e.g., a diagnostic system update from a manufacturer to its dealers transmitted via the Internet, in order to insert malware into the transmission, then the hacker arguably violates the Wiretap Act.

Intercepting transmissions from a vehicle also would violate the Wiretap Act. The act excepts from coverage certain types of electronic communications, including "an electronic communication system that is configured so that such electronic communication is readily accessible to the general public." At least one court, however, has found that the ability for someone with specialized equipment to remotely capture data transmitted from a computer does not mean such data transmissions fall under the readily accessible exception of the act.

In an interesting twist, the Ninth Circuit found the operator of a vehicle monitoring system could not be ordered, pursuant to the Wiretap Act, to assist the Federal Bureau of Investigation (FBI) in monitoring conversations inside a car. *The Company v. US*, 349 F.3d 1132 (9th Cir. 2003). One feature of the OnStar system allows the system's operator to open a cellular connection and listen to communications in the car. A purpose of this feature is to overhear thieves after a car is stolen to aid in the vehicle's recovery. Upon FBI's request, a district court issued several ex parte orders to allow eavesdropping under the Omnibus Crime Control and Safe Streets Act of 1968. The court found the monitoring service fell under the definition of the statute and required cooperation with law enforcement officials. However, when the OnStar listening feature was engaged, it disengaged other OnStar functions, including the button for automatic emergency response. On appeal, the Ninth Circuit found the lower court order invalid because it caused more than a "minimum of interference" with OnStar's services, so OnStar could not be ordered to comply with the FBI request.

How the Wiretap Act can assist law enforcement or civilians in addressing the vulnerability of a car's ECUs is not yet resolved.

Applicability of a Trespass to Chattel Tort Theory

A cause of action for trespass to chattel, governed by state law, might hold hackers liable for their activities. Generally, the tort requires intentionally dispossessing another of chattel, or using or intermeddling with chattel in the possession of another with resulting harm in the form of property damage or diminution of quality, condition, or value. An Illinois court found the plaintiff's allegation of trespass to chattel by defendant's installation of spyware on his personal computer was sufficient to withstand a motion to dismiss. *Sotelo v. DirectRevenue, LLC*, 384 F. Supp. 2d 1219 (N.D. Ill. 2005). Therefore, this tort might be a valid cause of action to employ in seeking damages from a hacker.

The PATRIOT Act

The PATRIOT Act and its extension modified numerous existing laws to protect against terrorism. However, the act does not address specifically cyberterrorism via cars. The act addresses terrorist attacks and other acts of violence against mass transportation systems, which are defined as passenger vessels, railroads, intercity bus transportation, school buses, and charter and sightseeing transportation, but it does not mention private passenger vehicles or trucks. The act also added to the punishment section of the CFAA offenses that are "a threat to public health or safety," but it did not otherwise amend the CFAA. As a result, the PATRIOT Act does not directly address car cyberterrorism.

Conclusion

Car makers are taking steps to reduce vulnerabilities to malware and cyberattacks that exist in their computers on wheels as they continue to roll out new products with even more technology. Legislatures and judges also will need to examine how today's laws apply to damage caused when hackers or terrorists exploit these vulnerabilities. These challenges will not disappear, but they might spawn a new industry: daily antivirus software updates for cars.

Viewpoint 4

To Combat Cyberterrorism, Understand the Hacker

James Hayes

In the following viewpoint, James Hayes argues that we must take a proactive approach to cyberterrorism, rather than waiting until an attack occurs. As cyber security advances in sophistication in an attempt to thwart the never-ending threat of cyber attacks, a new methodology, threat intelligence, has arisen that targets the hacker as well as the hack itself. Cyber security experts now recognize that understanding the motivations and methods of hackers can go a long way in preventing attacks. Hackers leave "fingerprints" of their work behind—clues as to their techniques and their style. These clues can be invaluable as governments and corporations strive to prevent cyber crime. James Hayes is a British freelance writer and editor. His work has appeared in publications such as InfoSecurity Professional *and* London Business Magazine.

As you read, consider the following questions:

1. What is "threat intelligence" (TI) and how is it being used?
2. How do state-sponsored hackers differ from those who work on their own?
3. What will the future of threat intelligence activities look like?

"The human behind the hack: identifying individual hackers," by James Hayes, Institution of Engineering and Technology, March 13, 2017. Reprinted by permission.

Sun Tzu's counsel to "Know thy enemy" is a staple of cyber-security advisories, yet it is only relatively recently that security experts have been able to flesh-out our knowledge of hackers as human entities. Better understanding hackers' human traits as an aid to defensive security regimens has become subject to renewed interest by those engaged to protect threatened companies and organisations.

Threat Intelligence (TI)-led cyber-security techniques aim to gather, collate and analyse information about sources of offensive action, and identifying the human element of online adversaries is part of this approach. Data gleaned from a range of activities can be combined to build-up profiles of hackers (and hacker groups) to inform decisions around how cyber-security resources should be deployed most effectively. TI does not replace traditional product-and-policy-based cyber-security strategies, such as intruder detection, antivirus software and firewalls, but supplements and augments them.

At a prima facie level, hacker motivations seem obvious: probably stealing money if they are criminal hackers, probably to promote socio-political agendas if they are hacktivists, and probably cyber-espionage if they are nation state hackers. Gaining insight into the 'hacker as human' is but one factor in TI's overall aims and practices – one that has less to do with psychological understanding aimed at trying to locate, apprehend, and even rehabilitate Black Hat hackers, than to understand what their innate human characteristics reveal about their future intentions and actions.

"TI will help to understand the threat actors and their motivations," says Ian Glover, president of information security industry body CREST. "It can [also] be used to establish credible scenarios to test security environments. As organisations move to [a state of] continuous threat monitoring, we will be in a position to see what is coming over the hill, and take action to ensure that we are prepared."

We have "really just started our understanding of the 'hacker as human' within the last five years," says Jonathan Couch, senior vice president, strategy at ThreatQuotient; before then "there was little real understanding of who hackers were, what they were capable of, and how they were executing their attacks. TI, plus greater information sharing and transparency around incidents, now provides us with in-depth knowledge of how many of these adversaries operate." "Attack attribution," the term used to denote patterns that pertain to a person (or persons) behind attacks, and their motivations for attacking, is now one of the key elements security practitioners seek as they safeguard their enterprises, Couch says.

"The more we study threat actors, investigate intrusions, and share that information, the more the human side of hackers is seen," says Rebekah Brown, threat intelligence lead at Rapid7. "We have analysed a significant amount of information over the past few years on threat actors and actor groups. We understand how nation state-sponsored actors operate—including how they are tasked, how they approach their operations, and how different groups associated with the same nation state collaborate."

To profile hackers, targeted companies must have an adequate data set to identify the characteristics of an attack, says Richard Starnes, cyber security manager at Capgemini, "and to understand who could be targeting the company, and what areas of the business they may be aiming at." The increase in the number and degree of cyber-attacks provides more incidents for TI to base its deductions on, and attackers—groups and individuals—continue to be identified by their tactics, techniques and procedures (TTPs). Attack attribution is key to acquiring knowledge of "who" to defend against.

The human nature of hackers is revealed not only by the "fingerprints" present in an intrusion—e.g., a commonly-used password, a preference for a type of tool or action, typos on the command line—but also by the nature of the activity itself, Rapid7's Rebekah Brown says: "When faced with detection, a setback, or a security measure that kicks them out of a system, we continue to see the adversary regroup, retool, and attempt to press on with their objective. These actors do not give up."

According to Pascal Geenens, Radware's security evangelist, at a baseline level the human behind the hacker can be classified using two parameters: motivation and skill level. Motivations include financial, revenge, political, religious, ideological and ego. Skill levels range widely, from chancers ineptly using hack tools bought off the Dark Net, to groups and individuals with advanced coding competence: both degrees of ability become part of their attribution signature, and help toward threat-level classification. "There is no industry-wide consensus on the taxonomy and classification of hackers," Geenens acknowledges, "but I am convinced that having a single, global convention would help us to increase our insights and use intelligence to prepare for, or prevent, attacks."

Recurrent, cyclical and seasonal shifts in the "threat calendar" provide another dimension to how the humanness of hackerkind drives their actions, often probably without their being cognisant of it, adds Geenens. "The gaming industry is a more likely target over holidays, and the threat comes mostly through motivations of revenge, ideology and fame," he says. "During academic exam periods the education sector faces a higher likelihood of being targeted by its own students—motivated by revenge or by a desire to cause disturbance to delay tests that they may be unprepared for."

The more known about the motivations and the human behind the perpetrator, the better their actions can be prepared for and anticipated, says Geenens: "Because we know the profile of the perpetrators, we know how to prepare for and prevent attacks. In the education sector for example, we know that the skill level of the typical perpetrator is low, so we can expect them to skim the Dark Web for hacker services." By monitoring the "dark" markets and forums, or by impersonating a Black Hat-for-hire, attacks can be prevented, perpetrators foiled.

"By identifying what kind of attacker your website might be a target for, a security team can craft a security policy geared towards that type of threat," explains Ryan O'Leary, head of WhiteHat Security's Threat Research Centre. "Hacktivists utilise distributed denial of service (DDoS) attacks, for instance, which target a site with a load of requests that bring the servers down. In this case, the targeted company would need to beef-up their servers, and be able to handle and recover from a DDoS attack." Companies need to shield themselves against all eventualities, O'Leary adds, but knowing who is targeting them allows for companies to prioritise what protection they implement first.

"Hacker profiling" is the process of assembling outline identities of individual hackers or hacker groups based on known intelligence combined with some expert conjecture. Often information that at first seems of minimal value later becomes part of the TI jigsaw from which outline identities are discernible.

"In the last decade, our ability to identify the profile and 'fingerprints' of hackers has grown exponentially," says Capgemini's Richard Starnes. "If an attack happens, we can now analyse how the hacker got in, review any code that was written, any language used or if a particular signature was used. All of this leads to generating a much better profile of who is behind an attack."

"Organisations are using operational intelligence platforms to ensure each step of an attack or malicious activity can be tracked and correlated together," says Matthias Maier, security evangelist at Splunk. "By setting up 'honeypots' on both the network layer, and in business applications and portals, attacker tactics can be followed and analysed to understand what is being used, and how they are trying to gain access. Based on what's being used, it can be determined if multiple attacks are associated with the same attacker, and then create a profile of them."

Understanding the motivations of a hacker can also help build threat "maps" which, in turn, can help develop a better cyber-security strategy, says Thomas Fischer, threat researcher & security advocate at Digital Guardian: "A politically-motivated hacker might allude to their characteristics through the tools and methods they use—for example, by using non-Latin character sets and encodings to avoid detection.

While knowing that a hacktivist might target your company because it is involved in fracking, for example, your strategy may evolve to identify specific threats—DDoS attacks, website defacement, data leakage—to your infrastructure in relation to this."

Understanding a hacker's profile, with specific reference to their individual modus operandi, and connections with other lone hackers, collectives, or organised crime, is very useful in identifying and predicting how an attack may develop, says Deloitte cyber risk director, Massimo Cotrozzi: "When the TTPs of a hacker or hacker group are identified, they can be used to assign attack attribution. This is complex and, in general, it is used to identify the likely group, by matching their TTPs and predicting where and when the next target will be."

As profile patterns establish themselves, organisations can decide whether a targeted part of their infrastructure, say, warrants reinforcement, or is likely to hold good in the light of continued attacks because the hacker's competence is not going to improve. The more skilled and advanced the hacker, the more unique their signature of attack becomes, says Günter Ollmann, chief security officer at Vectra Networks. "While it may be difficult to uniquely associate the methodology and tooling to an individual, it is possible to track by grouping to an entity. For example, the way malware variables are set, allocated, and flushed in the code, as well as the language compiler: all provide hints to the type of education and experience of the developer."

"Snippets of code or comments can, in some cases, reveal the origin of an attacker," says Rick McElroy, security strategist at Carbon Black, "but there is so much shared and borrowed code out there that it becomes very hard to say, for example, that a certain piece of malware we know was written by the Chinese Government was not further modified, and then used by another malicious actor. You have to blend all the available intelligence sources to attribute attacks."

"Hackers are humans, and can be both profiled and identified—drawing a picture of an individual hacker is possible, especially if the tracking activity is consistent and all information is correlated continuously over time," says Deloitte's Massimo Cotrozzi. "As humans, hackers also make mistakes, and may re-use assets, tools, and methodologies which give away their identity. At this point the hacker can be profiled from a social perspective. This could, for example, be by analysing the way they write, or how they code and co-operate with others."

"The information most valuable to hacker attribution lies in the infancy of their hacker 'careers,' as they're learning and leaving a trail of 'mistakes,'" says Vectra Networks' Günter Ollmann. "Later, they will make fewer mistakes, but their actions can be tracked back to their historical use of identities and mistakes. The best attribution intelligence sources lie in Domain Name System (DNS) records, web log, email, and message boards from past years which can be correlated to present-day events."

The same applies to domain name use, Ollman says: "For example, even if a hacker registers a domain with false information, some of that WHOIS data may be repeated from past attacks and configurations. Once registered, having access to the packets from the system that first configures the nameserver settings for the DNS provides insight. Even more so, the first DNS 'lookup' of the domain is almost assuredly by the hacker as they confirm their settings." These network attributes provide a unique "fingerprint," and often constitute "mistakes" if that data is available for TI investigation, Ollman explains.

"Hackers make mistakes, and we can see a trail of breadcrumbs that helps us to build-up a picture of them, their friend groups, and perhaps even where they live," suggests Carl Leonard, principal security analyst at Forcepoint, "and although skillsets can be determined, it is important to remember that the purchase of kits can make hackers appear more or less skilled than they may be. A skilled attacker can use a kit, leading you to assume they have nothing further up their sleeve, and then launch a more sophisticated attack. A less skilled attacker can use a kit leading you to assume they are operating at a certain level—but ultimately this skill has been provided by the kit."

Nation state sponsored hackers present different challenges for TI, but also have the potential to yield useful intelligence about the nature of the threat. The discovery that a company—even a start-up or obscure SME—is being targeted by a major foreign state can of itself prove revelatory, and remind the targeted party that the globalised Internet means anybody with valuable data assets will be found. Nationalist identities can often be inferred from tooling and methodology.

"Nation states do typically show consistency in what they develop and how they operate. Different countries have their own type of signatures based on targeting, tools used, and methodologies employed," reports ThreatQuotient's Jonathan Couch. "China has tended to be much more open in how it attacks others, and its methodology tends to be fairly consistent. Russia has modified typical cyber-crime tools that have come out of Eastern Europe. The US tends to highly customised capabilities. Iran has leveraged DDoS and social media in its attacks."

"State-sponsored hackers play in a totally different league," says Adrian Liviu Arsene, senior e-threat analyst at Bitdefender. "While in recent years we would only see one or two state-sponsored attacks a year, such attacks now surface at much higher frequency." Their modus operandi "often resembles organisational models specific to the military or intelligence agencies—they have research teams working alongside 'DevOps' and people who specialise in crunching exfiltrated data into actionable intelligence," Arsene adds.

"Threat Intelligence-led practices will continue to improve over time," predicts Stephen Gates, chief research intelligence analyst at NSFOCUS IB. "An understanding of threat actor goals, conditions for exploitation, variations of the threat, activities attracting the threat, outcomes of a successful threat, vulnerability indicators, and defences against the threat—all these are what strategic TI is designed to provide."

Going forward, Vectra Networks' Günter Ollmann believes it will become more feasible to build-up a composite picture of an individual hackers' probable identity, motivations, skillset, and socio-economic background based on intelligence-led monitoring: "Innovations in Big Data analytics and machine learning are making this possible. University research groups have been established to focus on this problem, such as the US Department of Defence's $17.3m grant to Georgia Institute of Technology to develop a 'science of cyber attribution.' These automated approaches are ideal for processing network data and binary artefacts, but omit the human intelligence factor needed for prosecution."

"Future TI-led cyber-security practices will be powered by automated systems based on machine learning and artificial intelligence algorithms," agrees Bitdefender's Adrian Liviu Arsene, "because companies need to quickly identify and respond to threats before they cause damage."

"While attribution is not a priority for all organisations, it has led to insight—sometimes new insight, sometimes just greater insight—into the adversary 'supply chain': what threat sources are developing and how, the marketplaces where they exchange these capabilities on the Dark Web and vetted forums, and the motivations that drive them," says ThreatQuotient's Jonathan Couch. "This awareness and knowledge allows us to exploit the 'human side' of hackers—to play on their insecurities, and to predict where attacks may go."

Cyber Deterrence Is the Next Phase in Cybersecurity

Dorothy Denning

In the following viewpoint, Dorothy Denning argues that, as cybersecurity incidents continue to increase, world leaders should consider cyber deterrence. This would mean establishing clear boundaries and consequences with other states that might be threatening cyberwarfare. However, the author contends, deterrence is much easier when it comes to conventional warfare such as nuclear weapons. Cyber weapons can be used by individuals, terrorist groups, and smaller states. The author calls on the international community to band together to establish global standards for deterrence. Dorothy Denning is Emeritus Distinguished Professor of Defense Analysis at the Naval Postgraduate School. She has received numerous awards and was inducted into the inaugural class of the National Cyber Security Hall of Fame.

As you read, consider the following questions:

1. How large was the jump in cybersecurity incidents in the years between 2005 and 2015?
2. What are the three things the author cites that can be done to strengthen cybersecurity?
3. In what year did the United States bring charges against Chinese military hackers who targeted American companies?

Cyberattackers pose many threats to a wide range of targets. Russia, for example, was accused of hacking Democratic Party computers throughout the year, interfering with the US presidential election. Then there was the unknown attacker who, on a single October day, used thousands of internet-connected devices, such as digital video recorders and cameras compromised by Mirai malware, to take down several high-profile websites, including Twitter.

From 2005 to 2015, federal agencies reported a 1,300 percent jump in cybersecurity incidents. Clearly, we need better ways of addressing this broad category of threats. Some of us in the cybersecurity field are asking whether cyber deterrence might help.

Deterrence focuses on making potential adversaries think twice about attacking, forcing them to consider the costs of doing so, as well as the consequences that might come from a counterattack. There are two main principles of deterrence. The first, denial, involves convincing would-be attackers that they won't succeed, at least without enormous effort and cost beyond what they are willing to invest. The second is punishment: Making sure the adversaries know there will be a strong response that might inflict more harm than they are willing to bear.

For decades, deterrence has effectively countered the threat of nuclear weapons. Can we achieve similar results against cyber weapons?

Why Cyber Deterrence Is Hard

Nuclear deterrence works because few countries have nuclear weapons or the significant resources needed to invest in them. Those that do have them recognize that launching a first strike risks a devastating nuclear response. Further, the international community has established institutions, such as the International Atomic Energy Agency, and agreements, such as the Treaty on the Non-Proliferation of Nuclear Weapons, to counter the catastrophic threat nuclear weapons pose.

Cyber weapons are nothing like nuclear ones. They are readily developed and deployed by individuals and small groups as well as states. They are easily replicated and distributed across networks, rendering impossible the hope of anything that might be called "cyber nonproliferation." Cyber weapons are often deployed under a cloak of anonymity, making it difficult to figure out who is really responsible. And cyberattacks can achieve a broad range of effects, most of which are disruptive and costly, but not catastrophic.

This does not mean cyber deterrence is doomed to failure. The sheer scale of cyberattacks demands that we do better to defend against them.

There are three things we can do to strengthen cyber deterrence: Improve cybersecurity, employ active defenses and establish international norms for cyberspace. The first two of these measures will significantly improve our cyber defenses so that even if an attack is not deterred, it will not succeed.

Stepping Up Protection

Cybersecurity aids deterrence primarily through the principle of denial. It stops attacks before they can achieve their goals. This includes beefing up login security, encrypting data and communications, fighting viruses and other malware, and keeping software updated to patch weaknesses when they're found.

But even more important is developing products that have few if any security vulnerabilities when they are shipped and installed. The Mirai botnet, capable of generating massive data floods that overload internet servers, takes over devices that have gaping security holes, including default passwords hardcoded into firmware that users can't change. While some companies such as Microsoft invest heavily in product security, others, including many Internet-of-Things vendors, do not.

Cybersecurity guru Bruce Schneier aptly characterizes the prevalence of insecure Internet-of-Things devices as a market failure akin to pollution. Simply put, the market favors cheap insecure devices over ones that are more costly but secure. His solution? Regulation, either by imposing basic security standards on manufacturers, or by holding them liable when their products are used in attacks.

Active Defenses

When it comes to taking action against attackers, there are many ways to monitor, identify and counter adversary cyberattacks. These active cyber defenses are similar to air defense systems that monitor the sky for hostile aircraft and shoot down incoming missiles. Network monitors that watch for and block ("shoot down") hostile packets are one example, as are honeypots that attract or deflect adversary packets into safe areas. There, they do not harm the targeted network, and can even be studied to reveal attackers' techniques.

Another set of active defenses involves collecting, analyzing and sharing information about potential threats so that network operators can respond to the latest developments. For example, operators could regularly scan their systems looking for devices vulnerable to or compromised by the Mirai botnet or other malware. If they found some, they could disconnect the devices from the network and alert the devices' owners to the danger.

Active cyber defense does more than just deny attackers opportunities. It can often unmask the people behind them, leading to punishment. Nongovernment attackers can be shut down, arrested and prosecuted; countries conducting or supporting cyberwarfare can be sanctioned by the international community.

Currently, however, the private sector is reluctant to employ many active defenses because of legal uncertainties. The Center for Cyber and Homeland Security at George Washington University recommends several actions that the government and the private sector could take to enable more widespread use of active defenses, including clarifying regulations.

Setting International Norms

Finally, international norms for cyberspace can aid deterrence if national governments believe they would be named and shamed within the international community for conducting a cyberattack. The US brought charges in 2014 against five Chinese military hackers for targeting American companies. A year later, the US and China agreed to not steal and exploit each other's corporate secrets for commercial advantage. In the wake of those events, cyber espionage from China plummeted.

Also in 2015, a U.N. group of experts recommended banning cyberattacks against critical infrastructure, including a country's computer emergency response teams. And later that year, the G20 issued a statement opposing the theft of intellectual property to benefit commercial entities. These norms might deter governments from conducting such attacks.

Cyberspace will never be immune to attack—no more than our streets will be immune to crime. But with stronger cybersecurity, increased use of active cyber defenses, and international cyber norms, we can hope to at least keep a lid on the problem.

Periodical and Internet Sources Bibliography

The following articles have been selected to supplement the diverse views presented in this chapter.

Christopher Beggs and Matthew Butler, "Developing New Strategies to Combat Cyber-Terrorism." *Idea Group Publishing*, 2004. http://www.irma-international.org/viewtitle/32381/.

S. E. Goodman, "Cyberterrorism and Security Measures" in *Science and Technology to Counter Terrorism: Proceedings of an Indo-U.S. Workshop*, 2007. https://www.nap.edu/read/11848/chapter/6.

Babylon Hoyte, "The Need for Transnational and State-Sponsored Cyber Terrorism Laws and Code of Ethics." *Forensic Focus*, September 28, 2012. https://articles.forensicfocus.com/2012/09/28/the-need-for-transnational-and-state-sponsored-cyber-terrorism-laws-and-code-of-ethics/.

Scott Jasper, "Russia and Ransomware: Stop the Act, Not the Actor." *National Interest*, November 19, 2017. http://nationalinterest.org/feature/russia-ransomware-stop-the-act-not-the-actor-23263.

Jason McGee-Abe, "Combatting cyber terrorism." *Global Telecoms Business*, August 7, 2017. https://www.globaltelecomsbusiness.com/article/b143pn16w1pxp4/combatting-cyber-terrorism.

Anant Mishra, "Terrorism in the 21st Century: Battling Non State Actors." *India Defense Review*, January 25, 2015. http://www.indiandefencereview.com/news/terrorism-in-the-21st-century-battling-non-state-actors/.

Alimorad Moradi, "Cyber Terrorism and Criminal Policy Measures to Combat." *World Research Library*, December 10, 2016. http://www.worldresearchlibrary.org/up_proc/pdf/576-148662350024-27.pdf.

Lt. Gen. Chandra Shekhar, "International Terrorism: India's Long Term Strategy and Concerns." *South Asia Terrorism Portal.* http://www.satp.org/satporgtp/publication/idr/vol_17%282%29/chandra_shekhar.htm.

Fatma Al-Wahaidy, "Worldwide hacking attack asserts cyberterrorism threat." *Egypt Today*, May. 17, 2017. https://www.egypttoday.com/Article/2/5281/Worldwide-hacking-attack-asserts-cyberterrorism-threat.

For Further Discussion

Chapter 1

1. After reading the viewpoints in this chapter, how would you define "cyberterrorism"? What types of acts constitute cyberterrorism?
2. Why do terrorist groups desire an online presence? What benefits does cyberterrorism have for them?

Chapter 2

1. Is state-sponsored cyberterrorism really terrorism, or is it merely cyberwar? Does this depend on which country is perpetrating the attacks?
2. Has state-sponsored terrorism been effective for countries such as Russia and North Korea, or has it been more threat than reality?

Chapter 3

1. Do you think paying hackers to regain one's data is the correct course of action? Why or why not?
2. What steps can be taken to avoid downloading ransomware? How can people safeguard the information on their computers?

Chapter 4

1. Do you think that "threat intelligence," the concept that knowing the hacker will help prevent criminal activity, is a valid field of study? Do you think profiling hackers is a worthwhile activity?
2. Should the auto industry be held accountable for making cars hack-proof and be subject to lawsuits if its products are commandeered by hackers?

Organizations to Contact

The editors have compiled the following list of organizations concerned with the issues debated in this book. The descriptions are derived from materials provided by the organizations. All have publications or information available for interested readers. The list was compiled on the date of publication of the present volume; the information provided here may change. Be aware that many organizations take several weeks or longer to respond to inquiries, so allow as much time as possible.

Berkman Klein Center at Harvard University
23 Everett Street, 2nd floor
Cambridge, MA 02138
(617) 495-7547
email: cyber@law.harvard.edu
website: https://cyber.harvard.edu

The Berkman Klein Center for Internet and Society conducts research on legal, technical, and social developments in cyberspace and assesses the need for laws and sanctions. Its website includes a wide range of resources including a cybersecurity wiki listing numerous articles on internet security.

Center for Internet Security (CIS)
31 Tech Valley Drive
East Greenbush, NY 12061
(518) 266-3460
email: contact@cisecurity.org
website: https://www.cisecurity.org/

CIS harnesses the power of a global IT community to safeguard public and private organizations against cyber threats. Their website includes blogs, case studies, newsletters, videos, webinars, and whitepapers on internet security. Papers include a guide to DDoS attacks and a Primer on Ransomware. A sample video is "The Expanding Attack Surface," which explores ways in which new technologies are increasing vulnerability to cyberattacks.

Cyberterrorism Defense Initiative (CDI)
Criminal Justice Institute
26 Corporate Hill Drive
Little Rock, AR 72205-4538
(501) 570-8000
toll-free: (800) 635-6310
email: cdi@cji.edu
website: www.cyberterrorismcenter.org/

The CDI provides comprehensive, transferable, and inexpensive cyberterrorism training to qualifying technical personnel throughout the United States. Classes are offered free of charge to technical personnel and managers working within agencies or organizations considered as a part of the United States' critical infrastructure. CDI is unique in the arena of cyberterrorism training, because the classes are brought directly to areas of critical need throughout the country, at very little cost to the participants. Their website contains information on countering cyberterrorism and other cyberattacks.

Electronic Frontier Foundation (EFF)
454 Shotwell Street
San Francisco, CA 94110-1914
(415) 436-9333
email: information@eff.org
website: www.eff.org

EFF aims to promote awareness of civil liberties issues arising from advancements in computer-based communications media and supports litigation to preserve, protect, and extend First Amendment rights in computing and telecommunications. EFF's website features an entire section of articles on state-sponsored malware and internet security as well as information on how to avoid becoming a victim on the internet.

International Institute for Counter-Terrorism (ICT)
Interdisciplinary Center (IDC) Herzliya
PO Box 167
Herzliya 4610101
Israel
email: ict@idc.ac.il
website: www.ict.org.il

The ICT is one of the leading academic institutes for counter-terrorism in the world, facilitating international cooperation in the global struggle against terrorism. ICT is an independent think tank providing expertise in terrorism, counter-terrorism, homeland security, threat vulnerability, risk assessment, intelligence analysis, national security, and defense policy. A search of its website turns up articles such as "Killing Lists—The Evolution of Cyber Terrorism?" "Cyber-terrorism, Cyber-Crime and Data Protection," and "Cyber-Terrorism: What Do We Do and Where Do We Stand?" It also publishes articles such as Cyber-Terrorism Activities Report No. 19 October–December 2016, which detail cyberterrorist activity for a given period.

Internet Security Alliance
2500 Wilson Boulevard, 245
Arlington, VA 22201
(703) 907-7090
email: admin@isalliance.org
website: https://isalliance.org

The mission of the Internet Security Alliance is to combine technology, public policy, and economics to create a sustainable system of cybersecurity. Members include major corporations such as Raytheon, GE, Thompson Reuters, and Starbucks, and universities such as Carnegie Mellon. The Alliance has international membership and global reach. Its members include Fortune 100 multinationals with operations that span the globe. They also include U.K.-based Vodafone. In 2018 it will host a global summit on cybersecurity in Geneva, Switzerland. Its media section has many press releases and articles on cybersecurity issues.

National Security Agency (NSA)
9800 Savage Road, Suite 6272
Ft. George G. Meade, MD 20755-6000
(301) 688-6311
website: www.nsa.gov/

To meet ongoing cyberthreats, the US's national leaders, military leaders, policy makers, and law enforcement personnel must understand who their adversaries are; where they are; and what their capabilities, plans, and intentions are. At the same time, they must ensure that the US protects its own national security information from those who would do harm. These are the capabilities that the National Security Agency provides to the nation, to its leaders, and to its fellow Americans—24 hours a day, seven days a week.

Organization of American States (OAS)
200 17th Street NW
Washington, DC 20006
(202) 370-5000
website: www.oas.org/en/

The OAS (or OEA) is a continental organization founded in April 1948 for the purposes of regional solidarity and cooperation among its member states. The organization was established in order to achieve among its member states—as stipulated in Article 1 of the Charter—"an order of peace and justice, to promote their solidarity, to strengthen their collaboration, and to defend their sovereignty, their territorial integrity, and their independence." The OSA promotes cybersecurity measures and educates its member nations about terrorism—both on- and offline. Its "Inter-American Portal on Cyber Crime" contains useful cyber-crime-related links.

Wired Safety
96 Linwood Plaza, #417
Ft. Lee, New Jersey 07024-3701
(201) 463-8663
email: askparry@wiredsafety.org
website: www.wiredsafety.com/

Wired Safety was the first online safety, education, and help group in the world. It began in 1995 as a group of volunteers rating websites and helping victims of cyberharassment. It now provides one-to-one help, resources and extensive information, and education to cyberspace users of all ages on a myriad of internet and interactive technology safety, privacy, and security issues. These services are offered through a worldwide organization comprised entirely of unpaid volunteers who administer specialized websites, resources, and programs. Wired Safety's programs and sites include StopCyberbullying.org, POSTitPositive.com, WiredCops.org, Teenangels.org, and Tweenangels.org. Wired Safety testified before the US Congress years ago about the risk to US and other teens being recruited online and seduced into supporting terrorism, gangs, and radicalization groups.

Bibliography of Books

Babak Akhgar and Ben Brewster, *Combatting Cybercrime and Cyberterrorism: Challenges, Trends and Priorities*. New York, NY: Springer, 2016.

David V. Canter, *The Faces of Terrorism: Multidisciplinary Perspectives*. Chichester, UK: Wiley-Blackwell, 2009.

Thomas M. Chen, *Cyberterrorism After Stuxnet*. Carlisle, PA: US Army War College Press, 2014.

Thomas M. Chen, Lee Jarvis, and Stuart Keith Macdonald, *Cyberterrorism: Understanding, Assessment, and Response*. New York, NY: Springer, 2014.

Jacqueline Ching, *Cyberterrorism*. New York, NY: Rosen Publishing Group, 2010.

Scott Jasper, *Strategic Cyber Deterrence: The Active Cyber Defense Option*. Lanham, MD: Rowman & Littlefield Publishers, 2017.

Allan Liska and Tim Gallo, *Ransomware: Defending Against Digital Extortion*. Sebastopol, CA: O'Reilly Media. 2017.

Malcolm W. Nance, Chris Sampson, and Ali H. Soufan, *Hacking ISIS: How to Destroy the Cyber Jihad*. New York, NY: Skyhorse Publishing, 2017.

Pardis Moslemzadeh Tehrani, *Cyberterrorism: The Legal and Enforcement Issues*. London, UK: World Scientific Publishing Europe Ltd., 2017.

Dhanya Thakkar, *Preventing Digital Extortion: Mitigate Ransomware, Ddos, and Other Cyber-Extortion Attacks*. Birmingham, UK: Packt Publishing Limited, 2017.

Dan Verton, *Black Ice: The Invisible Threat of Cyber-Terrorism*. New York, NY: McGraw-Hill/Osborne, 2003.

Clay Wilson, *Computer Attack and Cyberterrorism*. New York, NY: Nova Science Publishers, 2009.

Index

D

E

G

H

I

P

R

S

T

U

W